"Wow, what a gr~~...~~ ...utreach pastor, I have counseled many people dealing with problems that have all been addressed by these twenty-five truths. We all could have avoided mistakes in our lives had we followed these truths consistently. Ed has done a great job using scripture, famous quotes, and his own personal stories to illustrate each truth. I believe this book is a must-read, whether you have it all together or if your life is falling apart. We could all use the wisdom that we will gain from Ed and begin applying it to our everyday lives."

Brent Reeter

Outreach Pastor, Cornerstone Church
Chillicothe, MO

"I think this book will be a success and those who read it and apply its messages will be enriched physically, mentally, emotionally, and most importantly, spiritually. I believe the hand of God is upon it and its author, Ed Douglas."

Rose Lee Davis

English Teacher, Retired
Chillicothe High School
Chillicothe, MO

"Truth number nine in Ed Douglas's new book is 'Remember, little things can make a big difference.' This truth applies not only to life, but also to Ed's book itself. Ed has zeroed in on the truths that are practiced by the happiest, most satisfied, and most fulfilled people among us and has wrapped them in a concise, powerful package. This is a great read that reminds us of what is important in life."

David L. Sallee, PhD

President, William Jewell College
Liberty, MO

"*25 Truths* is an invaluable guide for anyone who desires to become a better person and to live life to its fullest potential."

Stan Shaver

Associate Pastor and Administrator
Word of Life Church
St. Joseph, MO

"*25 Truths* is an experience-tested guide to successful living for people of all ages, persuasions, and stations in life. In addition to being highly readable, it is highly believable in large part because the author, Ed Douglas, walks the talk. This book is perfect for group discussions in a workshop setting or personal meditation, or both."

Dean L. Hubbard, PhD, President Emeritus

Northwest Missouri State University
Maryville, MO

"It is my privilege to recommend *25 Truths*. Ed is a shining example and a wonderful mentor of life skills. My two sons are better people because of Ed's influence. The truths in this book are proven out in a life well lived. I have a multi-layered relationship with Ed. He was my banker. I am his pastor. My sons played on his tennis team. Now, Ed's son is serving as an intern at my church. Ed's truths are more than theories; they are proven principles. Everyone will greatly benefit from reading and applying these truths."

Stan Saunders, Pastor

Cornerstone Church
Chillicothe, MO

Ed Douglas has done us all great service in writing '25 Truths: Winning Wisdom for a Better Life.' Written with fatherly care, Ed shares simple yet profound truths that are greatly needed in a day when common sense is not so common, and basic values have often fallen by the wayside. I not only love the content of '25 Truths,' but I greatly appreciate the spirit in which Ed writes. He is not 'preachy,' but you can sense genuine concern that the reader grasps the keys to better and higher living. Ed's coaching background also shines through his writing as he challenges us all to become the best that we can be and experience the best life that God has for each one of us. Ed, God bless you, and congratulations on a great book!

Tony Cooke
Bible Teacher and Author
www.tonycooke.org

We have used the 25 Truths book as a guide for the State FFA Officer year. The chapters have given the officer team topics to discuss before each of our regular meetings. The officers have commented that the content or truths were a good reminder of what we should be doing in our lives and how as state officers we should try to instill these truths in the students that we meet during our year as a role model to our FFA members.

Keith Dietzschold
Missouri FFA Executive Secretary

25

TRUTHS

Life Principles of the Happiest
&
Most Successful Among Us

Ed Douglas

I would like to dedicate this book to the many people
in my life who have influenced me in positive ways:
my parents, Mr. and Mrs. Richard Douglas; my brother,
Richard; all of my current and former teachers, pastors,
and friends; and especially my immediate family, including
my three children, Jared, Aaron, and Kaylee; Aaron's wife,
Micah, their daughter London Beth, (our granddaughter);
and, most importantly, my wife Marla whose
encouragement and support have
made this book possible.

25 Truths:
Life Principles of the Happiest & Most Successful Among Us

ISBN 13: 978-1-60683-423-7
Copyright © 2012 by Ed Douglas
ed@eddouglas.com
www.eddouglas.com

Published by Harrison House Publishers
P.O. Box 35035
Tulsa, Oklahoma 74153
www.harrisonhouse.com

Table of Contents

Foreword

I first became aware of Ed Douglas's twenty-five truths in 2008. At that time, it was a three page list that Ed had compiled and titled "Life's Truths" or "25 Tips for an Enjoyable Life." He shared the list with friends, acquaintances, and students that he coached as the head high school tennis coach.

As Ed coached the team, he sought to get to know each of the boys and to share the insight of his twenty-five truths with them. At the time, my family was a Rotary International host family for a German foreign exchange student who played on Ed's tennis team. I knew from dinner table discussions with our exchange student that at each daily practice Ed would introduce a new truth to the players and quiz them on the previous day's truth. Through this repetition, he worked his way through the list, simultaneously teaching a lifetime sport and a life fulfilling lesson. He was not only teaching the young men how to improve their backhand, he was helping them strengthen their character.

Our dinner table talks turned into reviews and discussions of Ed's list. Several times over the last few years the list has come up in discussion and all our selected truths have been reinforced as dictated by particular life situations. I had a copy of the list on my desk for quite some time before finally moving it to a file folder and each of our grandchildren has a copy. If you sort through the materials in our kitchen, you will find a copy there, too.

In 2008, Ed shared his list with the Chillicothe leadership class. It was about that time that I began to encourage him to make the twenty-five truths his third book. It took repeated encouragement over the last two years to get Ed to develop his list into the book you are holding today. I encouraged Ed because I believed his ideas had value, I believed he was a true example of the type of success that is achievable through living and practicing the twenty-five truths, and I believed the twenty-five truths needed to be shared widely.

In your hands you have the twenty-five truths. Now, what do you do? Read them, share them, discuss them, and live them! This book can be a blueprint for you as it has been for many others. If you allow it, this book will help you live a successful life.

—Steve Holt, Director
Northwest Missouri State University Small Business and
Technology Development Center
Chillicothe, Missouri

Preface

One Saturday morning, a young father was trying to work at home but his son kept competing for his attention. Frustrated, the father took a section of the newspaper that showed a map of the world and tore it into puzzle pieces. He then challenged his son to put the map together. In a surprisingly short amount of time, the son returned with the task completed. When the father asked how he had put the map together so quickly, the son replied that on the back of the map was a picture of a man and he figured that if he put the man together the world would fall into place. In years past, I reflected on the wisdom that I've gained as I've gotten older and came to the realization that there are a number of what could be called "life's truths" that I wish I had understood much earlier. It is my belief that understanding and practicing these truths can help put the "man" together one person at a time so that, together, we can help the world fall into place.

When I was a junior in high school, I accepted Christ into my heart and my whole life changed. Prior to my commitment to Christ I had very little motivation, no real set of standards, and was satisfied with just trying to get by. After accepting Christ in my life, I experienced a new confidence in God's love for me which led me to want to do my best in all of my endeavors In college I had many good and enjoyable experiences, including individual and team conference tennis championships, earning nearly straight A's with a double major in math and English, and serving as student body president. The president of the school even took me under his wing and helped get me a summer job traveling around the country with the Kansas City Royals baseball team taking statistics for them. Later, he helped me find an opportunity to be a management trainee at a bank with a near promise for an opportunity to be the president of the bank.

From that point forward, my life has been one blessing after another. I had a rewarding banking career, lots of opportunities to be involved in civic affairs, the chance to write books and give seminars, and most importantly, a wonderful wife, three great children, a great daughter in law, and a wonderful grandchild, all of whom I am very proud of. I have really been blessed with a wonderful life.

Several years ago, while reflecting on my experiences, it occurred to me that the truth's I recognize in life have influenced me in a positive way that I understand much better and more completely now than I did when I was younger. Inspired by that reflection, I wrote a list of twenty-five concepts, what I call life's truths. My initial thought was that these were concepts I wanted to share or pass on to my children and someday grandchildren. Later, I decided to share these important concepts with the thirty kids who I coach on the high school tennis team because they are my kids, too.

Each day, the players and I would talk about a new truth and then we would review the ones we had previously discussed to reinforce them. The teenagers seemed to enjoy discussing these ideas and how they affected their own lives and they also seemed to remember the concepts well enough to employ them day to day. Recently, a friend of mine was housing a foreign exchange student who played on the team and he saw my list. He liked it so much that he told me I should make a book out of it so even more people could benefit. That is exactly what I have done.

This list is not meant to be a substitute for the great biblical wisdom of the Ten Commandments, Jesus' Great Commandments of "Love your God with all your heart and all your soul and all your mind. . ." and "love your neighbor as yourself," Matthew 22:37-39, the Golden Rule: ". . .do to others what you would have them do to you," Matthew 7:12, or other famous pieces of spiritual, moral, or ethical advice. Rather, this is my list of twenty-five tips that through my life experience I have come to believe will help you lead a fuller, better life. I think that the sooner you understand and accept life's truths the better off you will be.

My hope is that these concepts will resonate with you and that you can use them to facilitate discussions with your own children or others with whom you come in contact. Coaches and teachers can use these in similar ways to help their students and players. I hope that students and young adults can use my experiences as a jumping off point to discuss and develop their own morals, values, and ethics. Take it one truth at a time and talk about real examples from your life whenever possible. Look for real life opportunities to reinforce them and tell each other how they're working in your life.

If you're a parent, ask your children what they think and what experiences they have had, both positive and negative, with kids who practice opposite behaviors. Student-to-student discussion led by coaches and teachers can also be helpful and should lead to jotting down thoughts and experiences regarding each truth that will help reinforce the lesson. Finally, I encourage you to come up with some of your own additional truths, as that can also be highly beneficial. At the end of each truth is a page for you to use individually or in combination with others to learn and reinforce each concept.

TRUTH

1

Protect Your Reputation

*"The purest treasure mortal times afford is spotless reputation:
that away, men are but gilded loam or painted clay."*
—Shakespeare, Richard II, act 1, scene 1

Your most important personal asset is your reputation which is shaped over a lifetime by your actions and words. Many people think that building and maintaining a good reputation is about doing things that will make people like you. That's simply not true. Instead, it's the result of doing what is right, good, and honorable in every situation. A good reputation takes a long time to build, but can be destroyed in a minute by harmful actions or bad decisions. Therefore, it is extremely important to carefully consider the potential effects of everything you say and do. By doing what is right, you will not only build a good reputation but you'll also feel better about yourself.

A number of years ago, I served as President of the Board of Northwest Missouri State University, my alma mater. It was an honor to serve and a very interesting and enjoyable experience except for one situation that occurred late in my seven-year

1

term. One day after a board meeting, a reporter from an area newspaper called me to inquire about the board's decision regarding our interest in acquiring surrounding property under the right of eminent domain. I recounted our discussion to the best of my recollection for the reporter. The next day, I read the newspaper and found that the reporter quoted me saying something I had not said. To make matters worse, the incorrect quote made me appear to be callous and uncaring regarding the affected landowner. Although I knew that I had been completely misquoted, others read the article and assumed it was true. Even my own mother called me to ask why I said those things. I asked the reporter to retract the article but she stuck by her story and refused to admit any inaccuracies.

The president of the school was a good friend of mine so I solicited his advice on the situation. He said that because he knew me and I had no history of saying anything like what was quoted in the article he had no doubt that I had been misquoted. When I asked him what I should do, he said he believed that in life we all build up credits, which he called chits, based on how we live. Since I had a good reputation, I had built up many chits. Therefore, all I had to do was cash in a chit, so to speak, and tell people I had been misquoted. He said that because of my reputation most of them would believe me and that would be the end of it—which is exactly what happened. It bothered me to use a chit for something I didn't do but that's just how life goes sometimes. Life is not always fair and it was just fortunate that I had chits available to use. If I hadn't had a good reputation, the situation would not have been so easily resolved.

Summary:
Your reputation is your most important asset. Protect it.

Workshop:
Protect your Reputation

Do you agree that this is an important truth? Why or why not?

What kind of reputation do you have? What kinds of things have you done in your life to build your reputation, good or bad?

Is there anyone in your life who has a bad reputation? If so, how did they get it and how might it hurt them in future endeavors?

Is there a time in your life that you've had to use a chit or wished that you had a chit to use? When was it? How would the situation have changed if you had a different reputation?

What steps can you take daily to make sure you're building a good reputation? What will be difficult? What steps should you take to overcome those difficulties? (List plan or steps) What might change if you do this?

TRUTH
2

Don't be Lewd, Crude, or Rude

"For want of decency is want of sense."
—Dillon, Wentworth Essay on Translated verse (1684) line 113

Over time it has become apparent to me that the standards of common decency in our society have declined. There used to be a certain understanding in the United States about what was tasteful, dignified, and appropriate and, conversely, what was offensive, lewd, and inappropriate. As such, there were boundaries for behavior and speech. Now there are few, if any, boundaries on what we say or do and, consequently, many aspects of our lives are negatively affected.

On a national level, political debate often veers off track from a discussion of ideas with respect for the individual and their office to name calling, personal attacks, and ridicule. When this happens, bipartisan attempts to solve our country's problems can become hopelessly strained which hurts every one of us. If we could get back on track and learn how to be respectful of people with different ideologies we might get a lot more accomplished.

On a more personal level, we are seeing more sex, violence, crude acts, and crude language in the movies, on television, and in the media than ever before. Even humor has changed dramatically. It used to be that humor was respectful, thoughtful, and clever. Bob Hope, one of the most famous comedians of the mid-twentieth century, knew the boundaries of decency and might have made fun of himself, but he very seldom made fun of others in a disrespectful way. Now, little is out of bounds for comedians and, consequently, viewers.

All of this has happened gradually, like the slow drip from a faucet that eventually overflows the sink. People have become used to rude and inappropriate behavior and they don't seem to realize the continued gradual change for the worse. This trend is worrisome to me because we are a product of what we put into our minds, especially early in life.

Studies done by the American Academy of Child and Adolescent Psychiatry show that the typical child watches twenty-eight hours of television per week and witnesses 200,000 acts of violence and 16,000 murders on TV by the age of eighteen. It also seems that repeated viewing of sex and violence on television and video games can lead some people to more violent, aggressive, and destructive behavior. Children are like sponges soaking up everything they see, hear, and read. Consequently, frequent viewing of sex and violence, particularly by children, can have long term negative effects. One journal article on the subject states that there is "unequivocal evidence that media violence increases the likelihood of aggressive and violent behavior in both intermediate and long term contexts." It also says that "combining violent portrayals with sexual stimulation is particularly potent at stimulating male viewers to be more physically assaultive to females." Garbage in can lead to garbage out. That is why it is so important to think about or fill ourselves up with "whatever is right, whatever is pure, whatever is lovely, whatever is admirable." (Philippians 4:8).

I learned this lesson soon after I graduated college. At the time I often played the guitar and harmonica and told a few jokes at small gatherings and parties. One night at a Christmas party for a group of teachers I added a joke that was slightly risqué. The performance was going great until then, but after I told the joke there was immediately dead silence. It had fallen flat because it was inappropriate. I knew better, but I learned the hard way. By making a tasteless joke, I also made a statement about myself that was not one I intended to make.

So what can you do about this decline in common decency? Examine your acts and speech carefully beforehand. Is what you do and say respectful of other people? Will it hurt anyone? Will whatever you have to say lower the opinion others have of you or hurt your opinion of yourself? Will it serve to raise others up or bring them down? Is your behavior and speech fitting of someone who God made "a little lower than angels" (Hebrews 2:7) or more befitting of an animal? Remember, decency starts one person at a time.

Summary:
Standards of common decency have dropped dramatically. The key to change is every individual daring to be different—gracious, tasteful, and considerate.

Workshop:
Don't be lewd, crude, or rude

Do you agree that this is an important truth? Why or why not?

How do extreme levels of violence, crude language, and sex on TV and in the media affect your life? What, if anything, would change if these levels declined?

Have you or someone you know accidentally hurt or offended another person by crossing a boundary that you didn't know was there? If so, why did you think it was okay to do/say whatever it was that offended them? How could you avoid this in the future?

Do you make a conscious effort not to be lewd, crude, or rude? Why or why not?

How can you use this truth in your everyday life? What will be difficult? What steps should you take to overcome those difficulties? (List plan or steps) What might change if you do this?

TRUTH
3

Watch What You Say, Do, and Write

"Keep thy tongue from evil and thy lips that they speak no guile."
—**Psalms 34:13**

In today's world technology provides us with the means to capture and replay almost anything. This is compounded by the allure of fame and publicity which motivate people to tell secrets and embarrassing stories about others. Ignoring these facts and being careless with your actions can literally ruin your career, marriage, or life.

On an almost daily basis we see careers, reputations, and lives of public figures ruined by the disclosure of their infidelities, derogatory emails, or videos of embarrassing behavior. Tell-all books are also quite common, disclosing all sorts of celebrity secrets, from steroid use to multiple affairs. I am amazed at how often supposedly bright and ambitious people are so lax in what they say, do, and write.

You may remember when former Governor Mark Sanford, a potential presidential candidate at the time, disclosed that he had engaged in an extramarital affair. Immediately, the press found and distributed damaging emails between the governor and his mistress. Sanford's presidential aspirations were shattered and his marriage, his relationships with his children, and his effectiveness as governor were all hurt.

Tiger Woods is another famous celebrity whose behavior, specifically his infidelity, has at least temporarily devastated his marriage, family, career, and reputation. Even if Tiger wanted to deny his behavior pictures, text messages, phone messages, and testimony from mistresses who were willing to share their stories all ultimately made it impossible. How could he think this would not catch up with him? It is almost inconceivable that people believe these secrets can remain hidden—they never do.

On the other side of the spectrum are people like Billy Graham. The tabloids would love to print negative information about him. Obviously he is human and therefore, like the rest of us, not perfect but he knows it's important to try to live life in a way that won't cause others to lose faith in his message. A perfect example of this is the fact that he takes a modest salary and lives in a modest house even though his ministry takes in millions of dollars for missionary work. He knows that even the appearance of impropriety could serve to negatively affect his ministry and he acts accordingly.

Remember, even if it just looks like you are doing something immoral appearance can become reality when the gossip wheel starts spinning. While working at the bank, I made a personal commitment to myself to not ride in a vehicle with a female staff member unless there was an additional person with us. Although many would see this as an old fashioned way of thinking, my feeling was that perception can easily become reality in the minds of others. If anyone perceived the wrong thing both mine and the bank's reputations could be compromised, so I just didn't do it.

Another easy rule to avoid this issue is to re-read any written correspondence before sending it and asking yourself, *Would I be embarrassed if this was read by someone other than the recipient?* If the answer is yes, change it accordingly. If the answer is no, send it. This rule can and should also be applied to phone calls, public behavior, and almost everything else. The corollary rule is that everything a person does, says, or writes will most likely be seen by someone other than the intended recipient. Therefore, avoid the disclosure of damaging or embarrassing information by not saying, doing, or writing anything you wouldn't be willing to let everyone know, read, or hear.

Summary:
Live life expecting that everything you say, do, or write will come out in the open.

Workshop:
Watch what you say, do, and write

Do you agree that this is an important truth? Why or why not?

Have you said, done, or written anything in the last six months that could be damaging if everyone in your life knew about it? If so, what was it and what can you do in the future to avoid possible issues?

Is there anyone in your life or a public figure who you look up to who had a damaging secret come out? Did this change how you felt about them? How? What could they have done differently?

Do you make a conscious effort to avoid saying, doing, or writing anything that you don't want everyone to know about? Why or why not?

What can you do to make sure that you don't say, do, or write anything you don't want everyone to know? What will be difficult? What steps should you take to overcome those difficulties? (List plan or steps) What might change if you do this?

TRUTH
4

Be Slow to Judge

"... or how can you say to your brother, 'Let me remove the speck form
your eye;' and look a plank is in your own eye?"
—Matthew 7:4

"Judge not, that you be not judged. For with what judgment
you judge, you will be judged and with what measure you use,
it will be measured back to you."
—Matthew 7:1-2

When we hear a story about what someone supposedly did or
said we often find it easy to jump to conclusions, judge them, and
then repeat what we heard or take action accordingly. However,
if we take the time to talk to the person about whatever it
is they supposedly said or did, it usually becomes apparent
that the situation was more complicated than was originally
assumed, or that what they said or did was different from what
was originally reported. By then it is often too late to take back
any actions or words that you spoke in judgment of them.

This lesson was reinforced for me through interactions
I had with one of my players several years ago while I was

coaching high school tennis. At the time, this player was becoming somewhat of a problem. He showed up late a few times, told me he needed to miss several practices, and was beginning to have a bad attitude on the court. His attitude and actions were starting to have an effect on me and I was finding it difficult not to jump to negative conclusions about him. I was considering coming down hard on him, potentially even kicking him off the team. Instead, after more reflection, my decision was to have a heart-to-heart talk with him to find out what was going on in his life. At first, he was reluctant to share with me, but finally he opened up. I learned that he was having difficulties at home and that he had a young child. These things were causing considerable stress, financial and otherwise. He was trying to work as many hours as possible to provide for his child while still managing school and extracurricular activities.

Once I had a new understanding of what was going on in his life, we talked about what was best for him and how I might help him get through his difficult time. Although I couldn't do a lot, just having someone understand his challenges seemed to change his attitude and performance. A quick decision to kick him off the team would have been the wrong decision and one that I would have later regretted. Instead, I reached out to him and today I am very proud of him and what he is doing. He has tried to turn his challenges into something positive and is supporting his family, being a good father, and working towards a college degree. Furthermore, he has a plan for his life to use his difficult teen years as a ministry to help others. Who knows what would have happened if I had just written him off as lazy and kicked him off the team?

This is also an issue that I ran up against frequently while I was CEO of the bank with a staff of several hundred people. On a number of occasions, customers or members of my staff came to me with complaints regarding actions or inaction on the part of other members of my staff. I made it a personal rule not to rush to judgment about anybody until I had talked to all parties and was sure I had all the facts right. Instead of immediately siding with the complainant, I always took the time to talk to the accused to hear their side. Most frequently the situation wasn't as clear as the complainant explained. Even when it was confirmed that someone had made an error, there were often underlying reasons or circumstances that needed to be understood in order to fully appreciate the situation. Had I failed to look at all sides I wouldn't have been able to address these underlying circumstances and the same mistakes would likely have been repeated. This was also important because, had I initially sided with the complainant in any of these cases, I would have undermined staff confidence in me by demonstrating that I didn't have enough confidence in their abilities and character to get both sides of the story. It is important to remember that until you have walked in the other person's shoes, you cannot presume to know what happened or why.

Summary:

Remember, by the measure you judge you will also be judged. Most times when a person jumps to conclusions regarding others and acts on that they later regret it.

Workshop:

Be slow to judge

Do you agree that this is an important truth? Why or why not?

Think of a time in your life when you were quick to judge a friend, colleague, or family member. What happened? Would anything have changed if you had taken the time to uncover all sides of the story?

Is there a time in your life when someone was quick to judge you? How did that make you feel? What might have been different if they had looked at your side of the story?

Do you make a conscious effort to get all sides of a story before judging someone? Why or why not?

What can you do in your life to ensure that you don't judge people unfairly? What will be difficult? What steps should you take to overcome those difficulties? (List plan or steps) What might change if you do this?

TRUTH
5
Tell the Truth

"And you shall know the truth, and the truth shall make you free."
—John 8:32

The typical thirty-minute television sitcom is amusing. Often, the plot line starts with a little white lie that has to be covered by another lie and then another, each more outlandish than the previous one. Sometimes the result is funny, but even in the sitcom world there are often consequences to lying which include things like a loss of trust and tarnished relationships. In real life these consequences are compounded because, unlike a sitcom, your life doesn't start over again each week. In the real world repeated lying would not be that funny and trust, friendships, and meaningful relationships could be shattered.

The best way to avoid these consequences is to simply tell the truth—always. Some people believe that although they should be truthful about important matters it is acceptable to lie about small, less important things. Think about this though.

If you're willing to lie about the small things, why would others have confidence that you wouldn't lie when it really matters?

This is something I saw over and over again in my banking career. I am still amazed and disappointed by the significant number of people who applied for loans but could not document their stated income which is needed to verify their ability to repay their loan. Basically, these applicants stated verbally and in writing that their income was higher than the income that was shown on their tax returns. In other words, they were telling me that they were willing to lie to the government by underreporting their income, but were telling me the truth. Needless to say, that didn't give me a great deal of confidence in them and I did not approve their loan requests.

This loss of trust is one of the worst aspects of lying because it's very hard to regain once it's been lost. A lack of trust can wreak havoc on both your personal and professional lives. My point is perfectly exemplified by the story of a former employee of mine at the bank who repeatedly missed work for what she claimed was an illness. We all believed she was truly ill until one of our staff members saw her at a metro mall on a day she was supposedly home sick. When we asked her about what she did that day, she lied directly to us. We could have fired her then, but instead we chose to give her one last chance with the understanding that missing another day for any reason would be grounds for termination. Sure enough, within a week she missed a day of work for what very well could have been a legitimate illness. However, since she had lied to us before she had no margin of error and she lost her job.

Like my former employee, people often lie to protect themselves from the consequences of their actions. My advice is to be careful not to do something that would put you in that situation. Committing to truthfulness in all instances will help prevent you from acting in a way that you need to lie to cover up.

Summary:
Without truth there can be no trust with others, and without trust there can be no meaningful relationships.

Workshop:
Tell the truth

Do you agree that this is an important truth? Why or why not?

How has lying impacted your life? Is there a lie that you told that you wish you could take back? Why?

Think of a lie someone else told you. How did it affect your relationship when you found out it wasn't true? How could they have handled the situation better?

Do you make an effort to tell the truth all the time? Why or why not?

How can you keep from lying in your everyday life? What will be difficult? What steps should you take to overcome those difficulties? (List plan or steps) What might change if you do this?

TRUTH

6

Don't Talk Negatively About Others

"If anyone does not stumble in word, he is a perfect man."
—James 3:2

"With it (the tongue) we bless our God and Father and with it we curse
men who have been made in the similitude of God."
—James 3:9

Every day we all find ourselves in situations where it would be easy to criticize someone else. Often, we give into temptation and condemn the other person. From now on, when you find yourself in one of these situations I encourage you to slow down and think it through before making a negative comment about that other person. First, ask yourself, *Am I judging and being subjective?* If so, keep the statement to yourself. Remind yourself that when you speak negatively about another person you are comparing them to yourself and elevating yourself above them by bringing them down. No one should want to build their own self confidence at the expense of someone else's.

Alternately, you will sometimes ask yourself this question and decide that, no, you're not being subjective and find that it is important to bring the negative behavior to someone's attention. In these cases, you should make sure that you are being as truthful and as objective as possible in your assessment and discussion of them. As a boss I sometimes had to address negative behavior and, in those situations, it was important for me to be factual and not subjective, especially in my word choice. For example, saying "Bob, you were late for work," is factual and much better than, "Bob, you are lazy and you don't want to work," which is judgmental and subjective. Although you may feel that Bob is lazy and doesn't want to work, that may not really be the case. He could have extenuating circumstances that are slowing him down in the morning that you know nothing about. Staying away from subjectivity and judgment preserves relationships and keeps you from bringing yourself down by hurting others.

I don't remember ever being explicitly told that it's bad to speak poorly of others, but ever since I was very young I usually kept negative comments to myself. This guideline was so firmly ingrained in me that I didn't even consciously recognize the trait in myself until the end of my college career. At the time, I was running for student body president and my best friend asked me what my thoughts were regarding another student who was running for a different position. For some reason, the person he asked me about seemed to get under my skin and irritate me, so without thinking I said something like, "I don't know what to think about him." My best friend said, "Gee, that guy must be awful." Confused, I asked him what he meant. He replied, "Ed, I have never heard you speak negatively about someone, so this guy must be awful." That statement crystallized in my mind what I had been doing my whole life without realizing it. It also reinforced the importance of keeping negative thoughts to myself. As an adult I still try to stick to this rule and when I fail, I know it and regret it immediately.

For example, a number of years ago when I was coaching my oldest son's ten to twelve-year-old baseball team I made a negative comment that stands out to me still because it was very hurtful to one of the players. On that particular day, my son's team had a playoff game that overlapped with a bicycle trip I already had planned. I knew I would be late, so I arranged for the assistant coach to get the game started. When I arrived, tired and probably a little irritable from my long bike ride, I saw that the assistant coach had put our least talented player on third base. This kid was really very nice, but I typically put him in right field where he had less of a chance of handling the ball.

While he was playing third base, there must have been at least a half dozen plays on third that all turned out badly. I noticed that our players kept throwing to third even when they could throw to another more talented player, so I yelled out "Don't throw it to third!" Instantly, I knew I had made a mistake and I felt awful about it. My statement indirectly said that the kid playing third base was no good. I knew the child must have felt terrible and, sure enough, at the end of the inning the child's mom came to the dugout and said she was taking her child home. I sincerely apologized several times and asked her not to penalize her child for my mistake and let him stay in the game. Luckily, she allowed him to stay and he was hopefully not too upset by the comment in the long run. However, it could have been much worse. If she had taken him out of the game who knows if he ever would have wanted to play baseball or another team sport again? I know that there are much worse things that people can, and do, say about one another on a daily basis but this example highlights how important it is to think before you speak negatively in any situation. Remember, what you say does have an impact on other's lives.

Summary:
A mature person does not need to elevate themselves by speaking negatively about another person. If you have to be negative about someone else, make sure you are also factual.

Workshop:
Don't talk negatively about others

Do you agree that this is an important truth? Why or why not?

Think of a time in your life when you spoke negatively about someone. Why did you decide to say the negative thing? Would anything have changed for the better or worse if you hadn't said what you said?

Think of a time when someone said something negative about you that was true. Now, think of a time that someone said something negative about you that wasn't true. Did you react differently in these situations? If so, why?

Do you make a daily effort not to speak negatively about others? Why or why not?

What can you do to stop speaking negatively of others? What will be difficult? What steps should you take to overcome those difficulties? (List plan or steps) What might change if you do this?

TRUTH
7

Don't Hate—Instead, Forgive

"You have heard it said 'You should love your neighbor and
hate your enemies,' but I say to you love your enemies, bless those
who curse you, do good to those who hate you, and pray
for those who spitefully persecute you."
—Matthew 5:43-44

"Then Peter came to Him and said, 'Lord how often shall my brother
sin against me and I forgive him? Up to seven times?' Jesus said to him,
'I do not say to you up to seven times, but up to seventy times seven.'"
—Matthew 18:21-22

Most of us have known someone in our lives who was
consumed with hating someone else. These people's lives
revolve around wanting bad things to happen to another person
and not much else in their own life matters. This is because hate
is the opposite of love and when you spend a large portion of
your time hating others it makes it difficult, if not impossible, to
love anyone. It is obviously a miserable way to live.

In our home, Marla and I have tried not to use the word hate,
particularly as it relates to other people. When our children used

to say they hated something or someone we corrected them by telling them that they shouldn't hate anyone. We felt that even using the word hate could be the beginning of hatred creeping into their lives, taking root, growing, and separating them from the life they would like to live.

While I was working at the bank there was a customer I dealt with regularly that was just like this. During our meetings she was always telling me stories about what other people had supposedly done to her. She would make mountains out of mole hills with every little thing and took any slights or oversights as personal attacks. Consequently, she became consumed with hating others and getting back at them regardless of the effect on her. Witnessing her transformation was difficult for me because it was obvious that her entire life was becoming more and more unhappy as she became increasingly consumed with hate. Few people ever wanted to spend time with her because the hatred made her so unpleasant and, consequently, she was left mostly alone.

What she should've done was learn to forgive. Just like God forgives us for our sins, we are asked to forgive others. When you choose to forgive you release the feelings that consume you. By releasing the hate you are allowing yourself to choose love instead. The process of forgiveness can be difficult, but it's one that helps you recognize that no one is perfect and all of us need to be absolved from time to time.

A number of years ago, immediately following the death of one of my grandparents I was expected at my mother and father's house. I arrived much later than we had planned because I chose to do something fun and unnecessary instead. My mother and father were both mad and extremely disappointed by my insensitivity when I arrived several hours late. From my parents standpoint, my choice was selfish and disappointing, especially during their time of grief. At the time I didn't fully understanding that the choice I made would be so upsetting to my parents. When it became clear to me how selfish my action had been, I apologized to them and, over time, they forgave me. However, my feeling of guilt and disappointment in myself simply would not go away. I still remember vividly driving home several days later and crying out to God, begging for forgiveness. Several minutes later there was a moment in which I knew that God was saying I had been forgiven and I felt an overwhelming sense of relief and peace that defies description. From that day forward, my understanding of God's forgiving power was much deeper.

In the bestselling book, *The Shack,* written by William Young, a man's young daughter is abducted and viciously assaulted and killed during a family vacation. The book explores the theme of how God meets us amidst our sorrow and the true meaning of forgiveness and redemption. In the book, God tells the girl's father that he (God) "wants to take away one more thing that darkens your heart." He says, "Forgiveness is an incredible power—a power Jesus gives to all he indwells so that reconciliation can grow. Forgiveness is first for you, the forgiver, to release you from something that will eat you alive that will destroy your joy and your ability to love fully and openly." Finally, God tells the man, "I want to help you take on the nature that finds more love and power in forgiveness than in hate."

Although the book is fictional, God's advice to the man is something we can all apply in our own lives. The ultimate unforgiveable sin might be forgiving a violent murderer of a person's young daughter, but people have forgiven even that. They choose to hate the sin but love the sinner. Surely if they can forgive we can, too.

Summary:
Hate hurts the person who does the hating, not the person hated. Learn to forgive.

Workshop:
Don't hate—instead, forgive

Do you agree that this is an important truth? Why or why not?

Can you think of anyone in your life who seems to be consumed by hatred? How does this affect their relationships with others?

Is there someone in your life towards whom you feel hatred? Why? How does this feeling of hate affect your daily life?

Do you make an effort to forgive people in your life rather than hating them? Why or why not?

What can you do to stop hating and start forgiving? What will be difficult? What steps should you take to overcome those difficulties? (List plan or steps) What might change if you do this?

TRUTH

8

Be Quick to Apologize

To err is human; to forgive divine."
— An Essay on Criticism by Alexander Pope

We are all human and therefore we all make mistakes and we are often wrong. Unfortunately, it is also human nature for most people to be unwilling to say they are sorry. People are proud and it hurts our self-esteem to admit when we are wrong. Instead, we often rationalize and make excuses as to why we did what we did. When that is the case, conflicts are often left unresolved, which can result in very stressful situations that may ultimately destroy relationships. It takes maturity and humility to apologize, but nothing goes further to mend relationships, diffuse conflicts, and make life easier for everyone involved.

In my experience, regardless of the cause or problem, if you apologize the person offended will be so taken aback by your willingness to admit that you were wrong that they likely say something like, "It's okay, don't worry about it," and the situation or conflict will be totally diffused. Think about how much easier this would make your life by minimizing conflicts, lost friendships, and stress.

When I worked at the bank, we had monthly board meetings where I called on each member of my executive management team individually to give a report regarding their area of responsibility. One month, I overlooked one of the executives and he didn't get the opportunity to present his work. Following the meeting, I realized my mistake and after I immediately apologized to him he forgave me. However, inexplicably, the very next meeting I forgot to call on this same person for the second time. It was highly embarrassing to make the same mistake twice, but rather than make excuses I went directly to him after the meeting to offer my sincere apology. I told him that there was no excuse for my oversight and offered to put a procedure in place that would ensure the same thing would not happen again. Although the executive was still temporarily miffed, he recognized my sincere desire to be forgiven and to rectify the situation and, consequently, he forgave me and our relationship stayed strong.

Being willing to apologize is not just important in your personal life, it's also a smart business practice to own up to and apologize for professional mistakes. For example, while I was working at the bank I sometimes had customers come to me with complaints. If I found out that we made a mistake I was always quick to admit it and I would try to correct the mistake immediately. Statistics actually show that if a customer brings a problem to a business and the business does a good job admitting the mistake and resolving the problem, it can actually lead to a stronger customer relationship. This same principle applies to handling staff, co-workers, friends, loved ones, and acquaintances. In your life, both personal and professional, learn to recognize when there is something that could have been handled better and apologize when necessary. It will go a long way to resolve the situation and improve relationships all around.

Keep in mind that saying you're sorry doesn't always mean admitting that you are wrong or that you are going to take action to change the situation. When I was CEO of the bank, I sometimes had to make difficult decisions that negatively affected my staff. Occasionally, these decisions would involve correction or, very rarely, termination of employment. Obviously I took those actions very seriously and tried to make decisions as fairly and accurately as possible. In those situations, it was possible to make decisions that were right but still adversely affected someone else. In instances like that when you honestly believe you have done the right thing, you can still apologize or be sorry for how the action affected the other person. In other words, while you can't and shouldn't apologize for something you didn't do or a mistake you did not make, you can still apologize for how your actions affected the other person or how it made them feel. It may not rectify the situation, but it could help soften the blow.

Summary:

Most people will never admit they are wrong but a sincere apology will diffuse problems quickly in your personal and professional lives.

Workshop:
Be quick to apologize

Do you agree that this is an important truth? Why or why not?

Think of a time in your life when you made a mistake but failed to apologize. How might things have been different if you had apologized?

Think of a situation in which someone wronged you but didn't apologize. How did this make you feel? Would it have made a difference to you if they had apologized, even if they couldn't take back what they said or did?

Do you make an effort to apologize for your mistakes? Why or why not?

How can you become better about apologizing when you are wrong? What will be difficult? What steps should you take to overcome those difficulties? (List plan or steps) What might change if you do this?

TRUTH

9

Remember, Little Things can Make a Big Difference

"You see George; you really had a wonderful life."
—It's a Wonderful Life

Two of my favorite movies, It's a *Wonderful Life* and *Back to the Future,* have space time continuum themes. I love how, in these movies, the viewer gets to see how small things like little acts of kindness can snowball to change the world. In *It's a Wonderful Life,* Jimmy Stewart's character, George Bailey, gets to see how his town and family would have been detrimentally impacted if he had never been born. His seemingly small acts of kindness literally changed most everything. It's not always so easy to see this in our own lives but that doesn't mean it's not happening.

There is a term called the butterfly effect that was discovered by mathematician and meteorologist Edward Norton Lorenz in the 1970s that explores this same phenomenon. Essentially, the butterfly effect is used in chaos theory to describe how tiny variations can affect giant and complex systems. One day, when Lorenz was plugging numbers into mathematical equations to predict weather, he noted that the outcomes were totally different than what he expected. After looking over the data, he realized the outcome was different because the numbers were rounded to three decimal points instead of the six he had used previously. He thought the tiny change wouldn't alter the outcome by much, but he was wrong. Put into practice, this theory explains that it is difficult to predict large, complex systems without knowing all the small factors that affect the whole system. He showed that seemingly miniscule changes can set something in motion that will have much larger consequences. In a 1973 speech, Lorenz said a perfect example of this would be a case in which "a butterfly flapping his wings in Brazil might set off a tornado in Texas."

A number of years ago, I received a call from my high school tennis coach who I had not seen in many years. He told me on the phone that he had taken a drive of over seventy miles to Chillicothe and, when he remembered it was my hometown, he decided to look me up. He had checked into a motel and asked if I could come see him. I was painting my house and had paint all over me, so I told him that it would be great to see him and that I would come as soon as I cleaned up. However, while I was getting ready, he called back and told my wife he didn't think it would work for us to get together. Sensing something was wrong, I immediately got in my car and drove to the motel, paint splatters and all.

At the motel, my former coach told me that he was an alcoholic and had just gone on a drinking binge. He told me that he was considering suicide because he had lost his job, lost his wife, and had a strained relationship with his children. He felt that his whole life was in shambles. During our conversation, he told me that he had made no difference in the world and everyone would be better off if he had never been born.

In an instant, I was provided with exactly the right thing to say to him. I reminded him of when I was in 8th grade, playing tennis at the local tennis courts and he came by and strongly encouraged me to go out for the high school tennis team, something I most likely would not have done otherwise. As a result of his encouragement, I went out for the tennis team and became a state high school finalist. That determined the college I attended because that college offered me a tennis scholarship. While I was in college, the president of the school brought a job opportunity to me which led to my career in Chillicothe as a bank president. In Chillicothe, I met my future wife which obviously led to our three children. I showed him how his one act of encouragement most likely changed my entire life. How could he possibly think he had never made a positive difference in the world? I believe my words helped him at the time and, thankfully, he did not take his own life that night. Our conversation helped me, too, because it reinforced how little things can make a big difference.

Summary:

Just as a butterfly flapping his wings in one part of the world can contribute to a hurricane in another part, the small things that a person does can make a big difference.

Workshop:
Remember, little things can make a big difference

Do you think this truth is important? Why or why not?

Can you think of a time in your when you failed to do something small that would have made a big difference to someone else? If so, what happened? How might things have been different if you had taken action?

Has there ever been a time when someone did something small for you that made a big impact? If so, what did they do and how did it affect you? How might things have changed if they had not done this?

Do you make a conscious effort to do small things and/or little acts of kindness for other people to make their lives better? Why or why not?

How can you start doing little things to help others throughout your day? What will be difficult? What steps should you take to overcome those difficulties? (List plan or steps) What might change if you start doing this?

TRUTH
10

Utilize Compound Interest:
The Eighth Wonder of the World

"Compound interest is the most important mathematical concept I ever learned."
—Attributed to Albert Einstein

A number of years ago I was inspired to write my first book, *Making a Million With Only $2000—Every Young Person Can Do It.* I did this because I believe students and young adults need to understand the power of compound interest and the importance of saving early in life. However, knowing the value of compound interest and saving is not only beneficial to young people. It's a vital component for everyone that can ultimately make your money work for you and help you live a wealthier, more comfortable life.

The main premise of my previous book is that a student (or anyone) can take 2,000 dollars and invest it in a high-quality stock fund within the structure of a Roth IRA and turn it into 1,000,000 dollars in approximately fifty-five years by taking advantage of compound interest. Compound interest is the process of earning interest or return on an investment and then allowing that interest to be added to the original investment so that interest earns on that interest and the return grows exponentially. This is not a get rich quick scheme, but a concept that shows how small amounts saved and invested wisely can use the power of compound interest to grow to very large amounts given time and a good interest rate.

An extreme real life example of this concept involves legendary investor Warren Buffet, who runs Berkshire Hathaway. In the early 1960's, if you invested only 1,000 dollars in Berkshire Hathaway you would have a return of more than 25,000,000 dollars today. In fact, the stock has done so well that it has been reported that there are over one hundred families in Omaha (where Berkshire Hathaway is headquartered) who purchased the stock many years ago who today have over 100,000,000 dollars of Berkshire Hathaway stock. This is not a typical example, but it serves to shows the power of compound interest, which Berkshire Hathaway tapped into by taking their profits each year and using them to grow the company further, effectively compounding those earnings. Unfortunately, we can't all be Warren Buffet, but here are some basic saving and investing tips that can help anyone become wealthier over time:

1. **Save regularly.** The discipline and regularity of saving are more important than the amount. As a general rule, it is ideal to save 2 dollars out of every 10 dollars that you earn or are given. If you're can't do that, save at least 1 dollar. The best thing to do is set up

automatic saving with your bank so that a percentage automatically comes out of your paycheck or account— that way you can't forget or change your mind.

2. **Start early in life.** The earlier the better. Time is an essential component because it allows the money time to grow.

3. **Save for emergencies, goals, and retirement.** The ideal way to save is to put away 5 percent, or 5 dollars of every 100 dollars, for emergencies, 5 percent for short and intermediate goals (meaning things like college, a car, a down payment on a house, a computer, a vacation, etc.), and 10 percent for retirement or a permanent fund from which only the interest will someday be spent.

4. **Invest in a good quality stock fund.** If you can, seek advice from a trusted banker or broker to help you invest in a well diversified stock fund. If you can't do that, research on your own to find a good quality mutual fund that invests in several hundred stocks for safety and diversification, or buy an index fund that replicates the overall stock market. As a whole, all the large and small stocks in the United States have compounded at nearly 11 percent over the last eighty plus years. Investing in stocks shows a belief in capitalism, our economy, and American ingenuity and know-how.

5. **Understand compound interest.** This is essentially the process of earning interest not only on the principal, but also on the interest you've already accrued. For example, if you have 2,000 dollars compounding at 12 percent interest, it will equal 1,000,000 dollars in about fifty-five years. If you save and invest just 1 dollar per day at a 12 percent interest rate, it will compound to over 1,500,000 dollars in the same period of time.

6. **Understand the rule of seventy-two.** The rule of seventy-two is a great tool you can use to figure the power of compound interest without a financial calculator. According to the rule of seventy-two, the interest rate divided into seventy-two will tell you the number of years it will take until a given amount of money will double. For example, at a 6 percent compound interest rate money doubles every twelve years. At a 12 percent compound interest rate, money doubles every six years. So, the longer money is invested and the larger the interest rate, the faster money can grow.

7. **Invest in a tax sheltered account.** Some of your permanent fund should be within a tax sheltered account like a Roth IRA. This money will be allowed to grow tax free, even at withdrawal. This allows investments inside this account to compound faster and into larger amounts without the penalty of taxes. Note,

however, that there is an early withdrawal penalty if you take money out before you are fifty-nine and a half.

Money won't make you happy, but not having enough can make you very unhappy. Managing your finances prudently can free you from money problems, allowing you to concentrate on fulfilling your purpose in life, one of which may be using your money and resources in a way that will benefit others. For example, through the Bill Gates Foundation, Bill Gates and Warren Buffett have used a great deal of their wealth (many billions of dollars) to work towards the elimination of AIDS and reduction of poverty in the world.

My hope has been that because of my previous book and the talks I've given to students many of them have decided to start saving early in life. I have the same hope for you. I am confident that developing the discipline of saving will make a huge difference in anyone's financial future, potentially making many new millionaires who will use their financial resources to help others and to better fulfill their purpose in life.

Summary:

Saving regularly early in life and investing wisely can turn small amounts of money into huge dollars that can make a person very wealthy.

Workshop:
Utilize compound interest: the eighth wonder of the world

Do you think this is an important truth? Why or why not?

Think about how much money you made in the last six months from your job, allowance, birthdays, etc. What did you spend it on? If you didn't save any, do you wish you had?

Talk to your parents or another adult in your life. Do they invest their money and take advantage of compound interest? If so, how has it been helpful to them? If not, do they regret not starting at a younger age?

Do you make a conscious effort to save a portion of all the money you get? Why or why not? If you don't save money, what things coming up in your life might you want to start saving for? (For example, college, a trip with friends, a new mp3 player, etc.)

How can you start saving more money? What will be difficult? What steps should you take to overcome those difficulties? (List plan or steps) How might your life be different ten years from now if you start saving today?

TRUTH
11

Take it One Step at a Time

"Slow and steady wins the race."
—*"The Tortoise and the Hare" Aesop's Fables*

Often really meaningful goals that you have for yourself can seem overwhelmingly difficult like climbing a mountain. The key to success in these matters is to take the giant task one step at a time. In this way even a mountain can be conquered. I would hazard a guess that the majority of the most successful people in this country got where they are today by using this method.

Radio talk show host Dave Ramsey often tells the story of a lunch he had with a successful billionaire. At the lunch, Dave asked the billionaire what his favorite book was. The billionaire responded that his favorite book was one that had made a huge difference in his business career and one that he read to his children and now to his grandchildren regularly—*The Tortoise and the Hare*. The billionaire said it was his favorite book because its theme of slow and steady wins the race rings true to what it takes to succeed in life.

Personally, I use this technique to excel at one of my hobbies, which is running marathons. (My wife and others think I am crazy.) When you think of the full distance, a marathon can seem like a daunting and overwhelming task. However, if you prepare by gradually building up your miles over an extended period of time, you can prepare your body to be able to handle the rigors of the race. Even with training, 26.2 miles can still seem overwhelming. The important thing is to not think of it as 26.2 miles. Instead, like other daunting tasks in life, break it down into more doable segments. In the case of a marathon, I take it a mile at a time and sometimes at the end of the race I even take it a step at a time.

I've also seen this technique pay off in my fifteen years of coaching high school tennis. Over the years, I've found it helpful to tell my players to think in terms of playing one point at a time. Focusing exclusively on putting the best possible effort into getting that one point eliminates the worry, stress, and consequent underperformance that comes from thinking too much about the match and its ultimate outcome. By eliminating the baggage of worrying about things they can't control, the players are better able to play their best.

The important thing to take away from this is that too many people don't pursue their dreams because the task seems too difficult. Do not fall into that trap. Take it a step at a time so you won't become overwhelmed by the enormity of the total project or endeavor. In this way, you will accomplish more than you ever hoped.

Summary:
Take life one step at a time and, over time, great things can happen.

Workshop:
Take it one step at a time

Do you think this is an important truth? Why or why not?

Have you ever used this technique to achieve a goal? If so, how might the outcome have been different if you hadn't taken each step one at a time? If not, how might things have changed if you had broken a goal down into individual steps?

Is there anyone in your life or a public figure you admire who you think has used this technique to get where they are today? Do you think they would've been successful if they had allowed themselves to be overwhelmed with all the work ahead of them?

Do you make a conscious effort to break the big tasks in your life into smaller, more manageable steps? Why or why not? Is what you're doing working for you?

How can you start doing this in your own life? What will be difficult? What steps should you take to overcome those difficulties? (List plan or steps) What might change if you do this?

TRUTH
12

Learn What Brings True Happiness

"We hold these truths to be self evident that all men are created equal, that they are endowed by their creator with certain unalienable rights, that among them are life, liberty and the pursuit of happiness."
—Thomas Jefferson, the Declaration of Independence, July 4, 1776

Many people believe that they will be happy if they can have nonstop fun. Interestingly enough, that's not true. Significant and meaningful activities or accomplishments that take time, effort, and hard work are what actually bring happiness to a person's life. Activities that fall into this category might be acquiring an educational degree, building a business or career, helping others, acquiring a new skill, building a relationship with your spouse, developing a strong spiritual relationship with God, or even raising children, which most parents may not typically call fun but a true source of happiness. Really meaningful activities many times involve helping someone else either directly or indirectly. As an example, a doctor has the ability to help save lives—a meaningful responsibility and true source of happiness. However, he must first acquire his medical degree which is something that takes a lot of time, hard work, and dedication.

A number of years ago, the governor of our state appointed me for a six year term to the Missouri Highway and Transportation Commission, a six-member group of three Republicans and three Democrats. This commission is one of the most prestigious appointed positions in our state because it makes decisions as to how to spend hundreds of millions of dollars each year, primarily for new roads and road improvements. Very seldom has someone from our area been chosen and no one from my town had ever been appointed to this commission.

My motivation was that this was a real opportunity to make a difference for our area and, consequently, I submerged myself in learning everything I could and participating fully in the commission. In our area, the main road is a highway that runs east to west and, at the time, it was mostly a two-lane road. One of my primary goals during my term was to influence the commission to make this a four-lane highway because four-lane roads are extremely important in helping rural areas grow and prosper as well as for safety reasons. In fact, a four-lane road shows a 70 percent reduction in fatalities compared to a two-lane road. Some of this two-hundred mile long road was already four lanes, but a forty mile strip west of Chillicothe was the critical next step that would most likely make be the deciding factor in whether or not the highway would ultimately become four lanes across the entire state. Our area had been trying to accomplish this for many years to no avail.

Near the end of my term, another commissioner and I were driving to an event with the commission's chief engineer, who is the CEO of the Highway and Transportation Department, and we both lobbied extremely hard about the importance of expanding this forty mile strip of two-lane road. He told us there were not enough funds and there were other priorities, but we both said somehow it had to get done. About a week later, the chief engineer called me with news that he had been in consultation with our congressman and there were going to be earmarked funds used to finish the road. I felt a definite sense of accomplishment that day because my role and my efforts served as one of the catalysts in a decision that would make a significant difference for our area. Just as we had hoped, shortly after completing the portion near Chillicothe the commission decided to expand the road to four lanes across the state.

In a blog I read a few years ago, Judy Warmington talked about how pursing things that can lead to true happiness often involves some pain because such endeavors are usually difficult and not necessarily fun. In my case, I wouldn't say that lobbying for the road expansion was a fun thing to do, but it brought me a sense of happiness and accomplishment when we prevailed. She goes on to say that once a person understands the difference between fun and happiness, it is a "freeing realization" that liberates them from meaningless endeavors like spending money, trying to keep up with their neighbors, or feeling jealous and envious of what others have.

When I was young I didn't ascribe to this idea. Instead, I tended to do only what was necessary to get by and didn't put my best effort into anything. However, when I started college I decided it was time for a change and I committed myself to giving my very best effort to everything I did. For example, during my first semester in college I studied consistently four hours every night. It wasn't fun, but the payoff was worth it. I distinctly remember finishing my last final exam that semester and knowing that I had aced the test which would mean I earned straight A's for the semester. This is something that had never been a remote possibility in high school and it made me feel great. Although my academic success made no difference to anyone else, it was meaningful and important to me. All my hard work paid off and led to success in accomplishing something I wanted to do. That moment my thoughts were, *I did it!* and it felt good.

Summary:
Combining your talents with hard work over an extended time to accomplish something of significance can help you find true happiness.

Workshop:
Learn what brings true happiness

Do you think this is an important truth? Why or why not?

List the three things in your life that bring you the most happiness (i.e., relationships with friends or family, special accomplishments, etc.). Do these things take work or do they bring nonstop fun?

Can you think of anyone in your life who would rather have nonstop fun than work towards something more meaningful? Does it seem like they are any happier than you? Why or why not?

Do you allow yourself to take on tasks that require a lot of work? If so, how do you feel when you complete them? If not, why?

What can you do in your own life to make sure that you are seeking out things that will make you truly happy, rather than provide nonstop fun? What will be difficult? What steps should you take to overcome those difficulties? (List plan or steps) What might change if you do this?

TRUTH
13

Make Every Day Your Best Day

"Today is my best day."
—City Slickers.

"Something good is going to happen to you, happen to you this very day..."
—Song of the same name by Oral Roberts ministries

Not long ago, my wife reminded me that I used to often sing the words to "Something Good is Going to Happen to You, Happen to You, This Very Day" before going to work. When I thought back, I realized that it seemed to help me start off the day with the right approach which helped make each day a good day. I probably stopped singing it because I got tired of it, but upon realizing what a difference it makes in how my day begins I started singing it silently to myself again each morning.

In his book entitled *Don't Sweat the Small Stuff—And it's All Small Stuff,* Dr. Richard Carlson has several important messages about making every day your best day. One message is that daily problems in the world and in our own lives tend to take on much bigger significance in darkening our day than they deserve. Sometimes these little things can be allowed to, in effect, take over our lives. Rather than remembering the important stuff such as health, family, faith, friends, purpose, and the relative prosperity of having enough to not worry about your next meal or where you will sleep, people let the fairly small events of the day dictate how they feel. In my case, when the stock market drops repeatedly day after day (as it did during the financial crisis of late 2007 through early 2009) it tends to sour my day—if I let it. The message of Dr. Carlson's book is that most of the things we worry and fret about are all small things. Consequently, if we can remember that the daily negative events of a day are mostly small stuff, we won't let them ruin our day. For me, singing that song starts my day off well and helps me focus on what's really important.

Another technique that helps me with this relates to the book of John. When I was a teenager, the book of John from the New Testament played a significant role in my own salvation. Then, several years ago during my prayer time it became apparent that for me to avoid sweating the small stuff and to make every day my best day, my daily focus should be on four ideas that conveniently make the acronym JOHN. For me, JOHN stands for *joy*, *organization*, *helpful*, and *negativity*, four items that help me focus on what is really important. Practicing being *joyful* every day can certainly by itself make every day a great day. If I don't stay *organized* I become flustered and experience unnecessary anxiety. So staying organized keeps anxiety and frustration from creeping in and stealing my joy. Trying to *help* someone else keeps you from dwelling on your own problems and brightens your day. Finally, *negativity*, particularly as it relates to other people, will almost always lead you down the path of a bad day, so not allowing negativity to creep into your thoughts or actions can save the day. For me, focusing on JOHN makes it nearly impossible to have a bad day and, consequently, every day is more likely to be a best day.

One other thing you can do is come up with a list of things that make you happy. While traveling to our vacation destination one year, my family came up with what we called the "best of the best," a list of life's special little things that we each especially enjoyed. All of us came up with our own "best of the best" list. My middle child, Aaron, who was around twelve or thirteen at the time, included fireworks, the Chicago Bulls, dolphins, and Dippin' Dots ice cream on his list. Mine included my mom's sugar "kisses" that she makes every Christmas, cherry Dr. Pepper, playing tennis with my kids, special getaway vacations with my wife, and buying new running shoes. Taking the time to make these lists made us realize how life's unique little pleasures can help make a day special.

Every day we each have a chance to let circumstances, pressures, other people, or events in the world get us down. Or we can choose to make every day a special day—our best day. I've learned to enjoy life and make every day my best day. You can do the same.

Summary:
Be enthusiastic, smile, be happy, and try to make every day the best day possible. An accumulation of "best days" will lead to a very happy life.

Workshop:
Make every day your best day

Do you think this is an important truth? Why or why not?

Think of the worst day you had in the past couple of months. What made it so bad? How might it have been different if you had approached it with the attitude that you were going to make it your best day?

Can you think of anyone in your life who has a sunny outlook and seems to try to make each day their best day? If so, how do you think that affects their life?

Do you make a conscious effort to make every day your best day? Why or why not?

How can you start trying to make every day your best day? What will be difficult? What steps should you take to overcome those difficulties? (List plan or steps) What might change if you do this?

TRUTH
14

See the Glass as Half Full

*"The optimist proclaims that we live in the best of all worlds,
and the pessimist fears that this is true."*
—James Branch Cabell, The Silver Stallion

"I can do all things through Christ who strengthens me."
—Philippians 4:13

Most situations or circumstances in life can be seen in a positive or a negative light. Just like the proverbial glass of water that is half filled, we must decide how we want to view them. We have all known people who, no matter what the circumstance, good or bad, seem to look on the negative side of the situation. Even when a good thing happens in the lives of these people they are convinced something is around the corner to take it away.

In my banking career there always seemed to be a few people (fortunately the minority) who would think of reasons why some idea wouldn't work or predict something bad would happen as a consequence of an action we wanted to take. These people were unhappy and unproductive. If they had their way, we would have never moved forward with any new ideas or initiatives for fear that they might fail. Other people choose to find the bright side of any situation. For these people, problems become opportunities and their future and its possibilities are unlimited.

In the late 1980's, there were a number of bank failures around the country. Several people in our organization looked at the situation negatively and saw it as a time to pull in our horns so bad things wouldn't happen to us, too. My philosophy at the time was that this was a golden opportunity to buy banks and loans from the government at very inexpensive prices. That is what we did and it turned out to be an extremely profitable move that helped us to grow from 100,000,000 dollars in assets to over 1,000,000,000 dollars in assets. If I had looked at the negative side of the situation our bank may not have failed, but it wouldn't have prospered so successfully either.

My retirement from my active banking career after thirty-two years was prompted by ownership's desire to go a different direction, away from our rural footprint and more into metropolitan markets. My approach to this situation could have been negative and I could have allowed myself to become discouraged or disheartened. However, I instead decided to look on the positive side of things and embraced the change with the realization that this could be an opportunity for me to focus on seminars, writing books, and pursing other exciting areas that have been enjoyable to me. Rather than contest this change in direction, my choice was to make it into a positive one.

My optimistic approach to this led to the best of all worlds because not only was I provided with a lucrative retirement package based on my significant contribution to the organization, I was also given the new title of chairman emeritus and was asked to keep my board of directors membership which allowed me to stay involved without having to handle the day to day implementation headaches. Shortly after I retired at the beginning of 2006, the worst financial crisis since the Great Depression occurred in the banking industry. So, as it turned out, my retirement timing was perfect and I was able to avoid the crisis. Had my approach been negative, the ultimate outcome may have been much different and might have created a situation in which everyone lost. Some of my friends think I must be a genius to have been able to retire at the exact right time. I'm not. Sometimes a person is better being lucky than good. However, in my mind, the approach of looking at the glass as half full really worked to my benefit.

A similar instance occurred in my life a number of years ago when I invited a group of community leaders to meet at my house to discuss long range planning for our community. During that meeting, our group decided that the addition of a YMCA in our community would meet many of the pressing needs we had, so we set up a committee to pursue that dream. Unfortunately, the national YMCA organization advised us that our town of under nine thousand people was probably too small to support a YMCA. This might have stopped other communities dead in their tracks, but we would not be deterred because we believed there was a need in our community and that we could provide a solution. Instead of giving in, our group saw this as a "glass half full" opportunity to show it could be done. Sure enough, our committee proceeded to raise enough money for a new, thirty-thousand square foot YMCA and a sizable endowment fund to help support it. Membership in the first year was about six thousand people—not bad for a town of only nine thousand.

After our YMCA proved to be highly successful, a number of other small towns in surrounding states saw what we had done and had the confidence to work to build Y's in their own towns. These proved to be successful, too. These towns, like ours, just needed to believe and look on the positive side.

Summary:
Be positive and look for the bright side of every circumstance. If you do, the possibilities for your future will be boundless

Workshop:
See the glass as half full

Do you think this is an important truth? Why or why not?

Do you see the glass as half full or half empty? How might your life change if you looked at things the other way?

Can you think of anyone in your life who always sees the glass half empty? What affect do you think this has on them?

When you're confronted with an issue that could be good or bad, do you make a conscious effort to try and see the silver lining? Why or why not?

What can you do in your life to try and have a more optimistic outlook? What will be difficult? What steps should you take to overcome those difficulties? (List plan or steps) What might change if you do this?

TRUTH
15

Never Surrender

"No one can take away your right to fight and to never surrender."
—*"Never Surrender" by Corey Hart*

There are many stories in history about people who succeeded only after overcoming multiple road blocks and repeated failures. They should all serve as reminders to us to never surrender and never give up. Many of these stories are familiar, but one that you may not have heard involves a person named Otto Rohwedder.

In the early part of the twentieth century, Rohwedder had the idea that housewives might like to have bread that was pre-sliced rather than solid loaves that they had to slice themselves. He decided to make a machine that would do this and spent fifteen years of his life building a prototype. However, before he was able to make use of his work, the prototype and all of the blue prints were destroyed in a fire. Around the same time, Rohwedder's doctor told him that he had a disease that would be fatal within the year and therefore he should go home, put his affairs in order, and get ready for death. Rohwedder chose not to take his doctor's advice and instead he started over with his bread slicing machine. Some ten years later, on July 7, 1928, he introduced the first bread slicing machine in Chillicothe, Missouri (my hometown). From that day forward, sliced bread was extremely popular. We've all heard the phrase "That's the greatest thing since sliced bread."

I know this story of perseverance well because I am leading a group in my hometown to develop this story as a marketing tool. We have approval from the city to make our city's official slogan "The Home of Sliced Bread." We also have a marker at the original site explaining the history, along with a display in our county museum, gift items at local merchants, a Web site, and an overall plan to build a new museum about innovation. Rohwedder's story—and the saying—is one that has become the standard for all innovation, past, present, and future, and also one that can teach us the importance of persevering in the face of all obstacles.

Another lesson in never surrendering can be found in Jim Collin's book, *Good to Great* in which he writes about Vietnam prisoner of war hero, Admiral James Stockdale. Admiral Stockdale was the highest ranking POW for seven long years in the "Hanoi Hilton" where he was unmercifully and repeatedly beaten and tortured over twenty times, starved, and abused. Despite all this, he survived for reasons that are now known as the "Stockdale paradox." Stockdale says he never lost an unwavering faith that he would ultimately prevail in the end, that he would come out stronger, and that this would be the defining moment in his life. Therefore, he never surrendered. The paradox is that while maintaining this unwavering faith that he would prevail, he had the discipline to recognize and confront the brutal facts of his situation—that it was going to be a long and difficult ordeal. According to Stockdale, the prisoners who didn't survive did not confront the brutal facts realistically which later caused them to lose faith, surrender, and die. This never surrender attitude is one that we often find in military situations like Stockdale's, but that is certainly not the only time it is important.

Persistence is also a philosophy that I often employ when I'm running in a marathon. One of the reasons I enjoy running marathons is because I believe it is a microcosm of life. It is a long, arduous journey with many ups and downs that require preparation, concentration, maximum effort, and, most of all, perseverance. More than anything, a marathon runner wants to finish the race. No matter how hard the race, nor how tired the runner, they always want to finish. I have finished all sixteen of my marathons, but not without going through stages of the race in which I feel like quitting. I've been hot, tired to near exhaustion, experiencing muscle cramping, and dealing with the hardest thing of all, the mental strain. *Can and will I fight through the pain and fatigue to finish?* It is important to keep telling myself I can do it. J*ust go a little further. Keep at it. Don't give up. Don't quit. Never surrender.* Conquering the doubts all the way through to the finish line is a great feeling.

In life, whether it is a job, school, a sport, or a relationship, it is important to never give up. As life's setbacks and tragedies occur, just like a boxer who gets knocked down in a prize fight, you have the choice to stay down and be defeated or to get up again and again. History is filled with examples of extremely successful people who only succeeded after multiple failures and rejections. For those people quitting or giving up was never an option. People like this have an attitude that, if life was a football game, they never actually lost a game they just ran out of time. Imagine what your life would be like if you had the same outlook.

Summary:
Successful people find ways to persevere and to never surrender.

Workshop:
Never Surrender

Do you think this is an important truth? Why or why not?

Can you think of something in your life that you gave up on too soon? If so, how might your life be different today if you had refused to surrender?

Think of a person in your life or a public figure who you look up to. What kinds of obstacles did they face in getting where they are today? How might thing be different for them if they had thrown in the towel when things got difficult?

When confronted with a task that is seemingly difficult, do you make a conscious effort to push through and succeed or do you surrender? Would your life be different if you took the other route?

What can you do in your life to ensure that you won't give up when the going gets tough? What will be difficult? What steps should you take to overcome those difficulties? (List or plan steps) What might change if you do this?

TRUTH
16

Practice—It Makes Perfect

"Failing to prepare is preparing to fail."
—Legendary former UCLA basketball coach John Wooden.

Before he retired, Larry Bird was my favorite basketball player. One game of his that I remember very distinctly was an important playoff between his team, the Boston Celtics, and their archrivals, the Los Angeles Lakers. With less than twenty seconds to go in the game, Bird made a three-point shot to take the lead. With only a few seconds left in the game, Magic Johnson brought the Lakers back by making a hook shot that put them ahead. With less than a second left on the clock, Bird tried to pull ahead by taking a very long, nearly impossible off-balance shot. It looked like it was going in but it didn't and the Lakers won.

After the game, reporters asked Bird if there was any discussion as to who would take the last second shot. Bird responded that "In that situation, you don't want someone who has taken that shot a thousand times, you want someone who has taken it ten thousand times and that's me." The takeaway point here is that the more you do something, the better you become. When you practice something repeatedly, whether it be a speech, a sport, a musical instrument, or something else, you can become very proficient at it because your mind and body learn to work together to make previously difficult tasks seem natural and easy. Like Bird, you might not always get it just right but you will always be the best prepared.

In a book called *The Outliers,* the author examines successful people and how they accomplished their success. In one conclusion of their studies, they state that most successful musicians and athletes are not just talented, but they also spent approximately ten thousand hours practicing their craft. In other words, equally talented piano players can be separated into groups of great, good, and average based primarily on the number of hours they spent practicing—in this case ten thousand, eight thousand, and four thousand respectively.

While I was coaching the high school tennis team, my two sons, Jared and Aaron, both become obsessed with being the best player in a thirteen-team district tournament so that they could qualify to play in the state tournament. The oldest, Jared, spent an entire year training to beat the two-time district winner. He jumped rope, took lessons in the off-season, played summer tournaments, and practiced harder than anyone else. During the season, Jared was undefeated until he lost a match against his rival a week before the district tournament. However, a few days later, he came back and beat his rival in a very close match in the district finals which was the match that meant the most.

Without his extreme effort and consistent practice that probably wouldn't have happened.

Three years later, his younger brother Aaron took a similar path to win the district tournament. However, in Aaron's case it was most remarkable how much he improved between his freshman and sophomore years. That summer, he practiced three times a day and we had to practically force him to leave the courts to come home for meals. The next school year his hard work and practice paid off and he went from the eighth player on our team to the runner up and state tournament qualifier in the entire thirteen-team district.

My youngest child, my daughter Kaylee, has shown the same kind or persistence in her dancing. She started dancing when she was just three or four years old and has practiced an unbelievable amount of hours over her twenty-four years. She attended dance practice several nights a week all through grade school and high school as well as summers and she entered a number of out of town team and individual competitions. She continued with her dance in college by taking additional courses normally taken only by dance majors and by trying out and making the college dance team. This has all paid off for her in that her college dance team recently finished fourth in the National Collegiate Dance Team Competition.

It is amazing what the body and mind can do when a person practices consistently at anything. Not only will you get much better, but practice can also minimize anxiety and nervousness because when the actual performance takes place muscle memory takes over and just does what it is used to doing. I don't believe I personally fully appreciated this until I was an adult coaching the high school tennis team. During practice my players regularly play against me. Although they are faster, hit harder, and move more quickly than my sixty-year-old body can move now, they almost never beat me at one of these games or even come very close. My consistency is just too much for them. Reflecting on this, it makes sence that they are not as consistent because, by my calculations, I have played over five thousand hours of tennis throughout my lifetime and they have played only a few hundred at best. Just more proof that practice really does make perfect.

Summary:

The old joke, "How do you get to Carnegie Hall?" "Practice man, practice" is funny, but true. If you fully appreciate what practice can do, you can excel at most anything.

Workshop:
Practice—it makes perfect

Do you think this is an important truth? Why or why not?

Do you have a talent that you practice often (i.e., playing a team sport or a musical instrument)? If so, what do you think would be different if you didn't practice? If not, how might things change if you did practice on a regular basis?

Think of a celebrity with a talent that you admire (i.e., a singer, actor or actress, professional athlete). See if you can find out how often they practice their craft. Do you think they would be as successful today if they had practiced half as much?

Do you make an effort to practice and develop one of your talents every day? If not, do you think your life might be different if you did? How?

What can you start doing now to begin taking the time out each day to practice something you're good at? What will be difficult? What steps should you take to overcome those difficulties? (List plan or steps) What might change if you do this?

TRUTH
17

Play to Win

"The only thing that matters is winning."
—Vince Lombardi

"Winning isn't everything; it's the only thing."
—Vince Lombardi

I am often amused at the attitude many people have towards professional athletes and even college teams. Our society today is consumed with winning. For example, a college basketball team can qualify for the national tournament with sixty-six teams, win five games, lose in the finals, and be called a loser. The only team that won in the eyes of many is the one team that won the entire championship. But the other team is still second in the whole nation. In my opinion, just getting to the tournament should qualify as a success and showing that you're better than the sixty-four other teams that were in the tournament is certainly winning. My point is one loss does not make a team or a player a loser. Instead, they should be judged by their season as a whole and also whether they played the best they could.

Like Vince Lombardi who is quoted above, many people believe that the emphasis on what a person does in life should be on winning at all costs. However, I think it's better to focus on playing to win, by which I mean that you should do your best by maximizing your preparation and effort in all of your endeavors. Sometimes, if you focus on winning too much, failure or loss actually becomes more likely because you can become diverted from the actions that will produce positive results, like focus, concentration, and even relaxation. Everyone will win sometimes and lose sometimes, but if you always play to win by fully preparing and doing your best you will never be disappointed or second guess yourself.

When I was a sophomore in college I ran for class president. About a week before the election, the father of a friend of mine, who had been in politics, asked me how I was doing. When I replied that I was worried and anxious about the outcome of the election, he told me that the important thing was to do everything possible to win so that I could awake the day after the election and say to myself that I had given it my very best. Then, no matter the outcome, I wouldn't feel bad. This advice helped me focus on doing everything I could do to win rather than getting caught up in unproductive worry and anxiety. I did win the election, but I know that even if the result had been different I would have had no regrets. What I learned is that in any kind of endeavor it helps to know that you are always a winner when you have done your very best by preparing and approaching the game positively. There is one famous athlete from my childhood who I remember that exemplified this perfectly.

When I was a very young boy in the early 1960's, I listened to the late Harry Carey and Jack Buck broadcast St. Louis Cardinal baseball games on the radio and became a lifelong Cardinals fan. I still remember attending my first professional baseball game at the old Sportsman's Park in St. Louis when I was ten years old and seeing their star player, Stan "the Man" Musial play. Although he was nearing the end of his long career, there was something different about how he played the game. He seemed to swing harder, hit the ball harder, run harder, and just overall play with more intensity than everyone else. It left a meaningful impression on me as to how a game should be played.

In 2009, sports writer Joe Posnanski from the Kansas City Star wrote a tribute to Musial in which he stated that to really appreciate Musial, fans need to understand not what Musial did but what he didn't do. In the over three thousand games he played, he was never thrown out of game, never treated an umpire with disrespect, never took his frustrations out on the field, and never treated the game or any person with less than full respect. He didn't take anything for granted and when asked how he was doing always used the word "wonderful." According to Posnaski, Musial also never turned down signing an autograph for anyone, which is something I know from personal experience. Many times when a favorite athlete of mine is on the cover of *Sports Illustrated,* I try to obtain their address and mail them my copy to sign. Some athletes never mail it back, but when I called the Cardinal's organization for Stan's address they assured me that he always signs and returns everything. True to character, when I sent Musial a *Sports Illustrated* cover he was on from nearly fifty years ago it was signed and returned in only a few days.

Musial is a hall of famer now and over 90 years old. In the baseball record books he is not first in home runs, hits or runs batted in, but many of the athletes who are at the top of those lists are tainted by steroid use and cheating. Musial always played by the rules and he played to win. His consistency was second to none and consequently he is in the top five all time in most every catagory including hits, runs batted in, runs scored, and extra base hits. Musial was beloved by everyone, fans and media alike, and as Posnanski said, "no one played with more heart." In todays world where baseball players put winning above all else and are remembered for their steroid use and unethical tactics, Stan "the Man" Musial is remembered for his character and how he played the game. I think we could all learn something from that.

Summary:
Always play to win. Even when you technically lose, you will always be a winner if you approach everything you do with preparation and complete effort.

Workshop:
Play to win

Do you think this is an important truth? Why or why not?

Think of the last time that you technically lost in a competition. If you were disappointed, was it because you lost or because you didn't do your best?

If you get disappointed when you lose, even if you do your best, what do you think you can do to change your attitude? Do you think this would make your competitions more fun? Why or why not?

What can you do to change your attitude so that winning isn't everything but playing to win is? What will be difficult? What steps should you take to overcome those difficulties? (List plan or steps) What might change if you do this?

TRUTH
18
Set Goals and Write Them Down

"Where there is no vision, the people perish."
—Proverbs 29:18

In 1979, some sources show that there was a study done at the Harvard Business School which is today known as the Harvard Business School Goal Study. On their graduation day, the question was asked of several students, "Have you set clear, written goals for your future and made plans to accomplish them?" The response from the students showed that 3 percent had written goals, 13 percent had goals they had not committed to writing, and 84 percent had no specific goals. Ten years later, there was a follow up study of the original respondents and they found that the 16 percent who had goals were earning twice as much as the 84 percent without goals. Amazingly though, the 3 percent with written goals were earning ten times as much as the other 97 percent put together!

Recently I have learned that there is a lack of documentation of this study and consequently there is some question as to whether or not it really took place. I don't know conclusively if the study took place, but from what I know about goal setting and written goals I would not at all be surprised with the kind of results stated above. Luckily, I'm not the only one who believed in these findings, real or fake. The sentiment of the Harvard study's findings has been upheld by a study done in 2007 by Dr. Gail Matthews at Dominican University in California.

Her study showed that people who write down their goals, share them with a friend, and send weekly updates of their progress to their friend are 33 percent more successful at completing their goals than people who simply formulate goals in their minds. The best explanation for this is that taking the time to write your goals out forces you to consider how they will be accomplished, which leads to the development of a plan of action. Also, when you write your goals down and refer to them regularly, they take on a high level of importance in your life. Having a friend to hold you accountable may also be helpful so that you don't get off track.

Despite the urban legend Yale/Harvard study and this documented one, it seems that some people still don't want to write down their goals. In his book, *Goals*, Brian Tracy says that there are four reasons why this is true:

1. They don't realize the importance of having written goals.
2. They don't know how to set goals properly by writing them down clearly and specifically.
3. They fear failure if they don't accomplish the goals.
4. They fear rejection if they don't accomplish the goals.

Written goals are nothing to fear. They can help you to decide what is important in your life as well as helping you accomplish those items of importance. For many years I have written out goals that cover several different areas of my life. It is amazing how, given time, these goals become reality. I've talked to a number of people who have also committed their goals to writing and, without exception; these people confirm that the vast majority of their written goals are ultimately accomplished.

Each year I commit my goals for the year to paper. My categories are spiritual goals (teaching a Sunday school class, reading the bible, attending a home group), business goals (seminars to give, books to sell, new clients to obtain), financial goals (amounts to save, important items to pay for, or home improvements to finance), family goals (vacations and special events with my wife and kids), sports goals (my tennis goals, running goals, and high school tennis team goals), and even number of books to read. I list all of these on a single page, which helps me stay focused on what I want to accomplish each year. Each day, my priorities for the day are listed in my planner and, ideally, my priorities and to do list tie in with my goals. Over the years, my experience is that I don't accomplish every single goal each year, but I succeed with most of them. For example, in my banking career, I set a goal for our organization to grow to 1,000,000,000 dollars in assets. At the time when I wrote this goal down, our bank was much smaller and many of my co-workers thought it was an unrealistic and unattainable aspiration for a bank headquartered in a small town. However, the goal proved to be important for our company because it gave us a long term vision, motivation, and something to work towards. Approximately seven years later we did reach one billion dollars in assets and we celebrated the accomplishment of what had once seemed an impossible goal.

My suggestion for you is to write annual goals for the main areas of your life that you would like to improve: spiritual, educational, professional, financial, family, or even athletic and recreational goals. Too many goals may cause you to lose focus, so be careful to not go overboard with too many in each area. Instead, choose a few that you think will really make a difference in your life. After you've written them out, develop plans to help reach the goals and refer to them often to keep track of the results. If it helps, find a friend or family member to send progress reports to so that you stay accountable. At the end of the year you should sit down and look at your list to see how much you have accomplished. I bet you will be truly astounded.

Summary:
People who set goals and write them down accomplish significantly more than people who don't.

Workshop:
Set goals and write them down

Do you think this is an important truth? Why or why not?

Think of the last goal that you made for yourself. Did you write it down and refer back to it? If not, do you think the outcome might have been different if you had?

Talk to your parents or another adult. Do they have written goals? Why or why not? If they do, do they think they are more likely to accomplish a goal if it is written?

Do you make an effort to make specific goals for yourself? Why or why not?

Write out your top three goals for the next year. What difficulties do you think you will encounter trying to reach these goals? What steps can you take to overcome these difficulties? (List or plan out steps) What might change if you accomplish these goals?

TRUTH
19

Exercise, Exercise, Exercise

"Eat a lot, sleep a lot, brush 'em like crazy, run a lot,
do a lot, never be lazy."
—"Mama Says" by the Beach Boys.

Most people don't realize how important health is until they're sick or in pain. Then nothing else seems to matter. Likewise, when a person who has been seriously ill gets well it gives them a whole new perspective on life. When I was a teenager, I had an illness that kept me in the hospital for two weeks. The day I was released I distinctly remember getting a Cherry Dr. Pepper from the Dairy Queen. At the time I felt like I had won the lottery because it was so wonderful to be out of the hospital enjoying a fountain drink

The best way to not get sick is to do what is necessary to stay healthy. When I say exercise, exercise, exercise, I mean, in a broad sense, doing whatever it takes to stay healthy and to live a long, productive life. This can include things like not smoking, not drinking in excess, eating plenty of fruit and vegetables, not abusing your body, and of course, engaging in regular physical exercise.

In a narrow sense, vigorous exercise has many positive health benefits. It is proven to help your outlook and attitude by releasing endorphins in the body that make you feel happy. These endorphins can actually produce what is known as a runner's high. Additionally, exercise reduces stress and helps you sleep more soundly and feel more rested. It also makes your muscles and heart stronger so you feel more vibrant and energetic. Finally, it burns significant calories which helps you lose weight or maintain a healthy weight and has significant health benefits like lowering the risk of heart disease, cancer, diabetes, and other diseases. I have certainly seen this in my own life. Some of the reasons for running marathons, playing tennis, and biking are already mentioned above. My other reasons are that exercising regularly and vigorously makes me feel good as well as helping me sleep more soundly and feel more energetic. When I have gone several days without exercising there is a noticeable difference in my attitude and energy level.

Additionally, growing research cited in a *Wall Street Journal* article written by Laura Landro shows that even moderate exercise of a thirty to forty-five minute brisk walk five times a week can "boost the body's immune system, increasing the circulation of natural killer cells that fight off viruses and bacteria." Conversely, inactivity poses "as great a health risk as smoking, contributing to heart disease, diabetes, hypertension, arthritis, and osteoporosis." Regular exercise combats these diseases and more. In fact, according to the same article, walking the equivalent of three to five hours per week can "reduce the risk of dying from disease by 50 percent." According to the chairman of Exercise is Medicine, Dr. Sallis, "Exercise can be used like a vaccine to prevent disease and a medication to treat disease. If there were a drug with the same benefits as exercise it would instantly be the standard of care."

Recent studies like "And Why More is Even Better," cited in a *Wall Street Journal* article written by Kevin Helliker show that stepped up, rigorous exercise can have even more benefits than the moderate exercise described above. Doctor Paul Williams studied 10,000 runners and found that rigorous exercise which greatly exceeded the recommended exercise guidelines "can reduce the risk of stroke, heart attack, glaucoma, diabetes, and other diseases by an additional 70 percent." Runners who ran thirty, forty and even fifty miles per week had progressively greater health benefits. A one-word theme developed from this study is that "more" is better for a person's health.

As we get older, it becomes difficult to exercise with the same intensity as when we were younger, but it's still important. I'm a goal oriented person so I keep all my running times written down from races and marathons. Times don't lie and I know that I have slowed down with age. However, I was able to run comparable times into my late forties and even ran my best marathon time at age forty-six. My times and actual studies confirm that after a person reaches their mid-forties, times slow down by about 1 percent a year or 10 percent a decade. That doesn't seem like much and it isn't in some respects. The real thing you should compare it to is how much physical activity you won't be able to do later in life if you don't stay active throughout your life.

Summary:
If there is a true fountain of youth, it is exercise.

Workshop:
Exercise, exercise, exercise

Do you think this is an important truth? Why or why not?

Think about the last time you exercised. How did you feel when you were finished? Do you think your life would improve in any way if you began exercising on a regular basis?

Do you know anyone who exercises regularly? How do you think that affects their life? Do you notice a difference in their attitude when they don't exercise?

Do you make a conscious effort to get some form of exercise every day? Why or why not?

What can you do to ensure that you get at least a little bit of exercise every day? What will be difficult? What steps should you take to overcome those difficulties? (List plan or steps) What might change if you do this?

TRUTH
20

Make a Difference in the World

"I expect to pass through this world but once, any good thing therefore that I can do or any kindness that I can show to any fellow creature, let me do it now. Let me not defer or neglect it, for I shall not pass this way again."
—John O'London, Treasure Trove, page 48

One of the most important questions you can ask yourself is *How can I make a positive difference in the world?* Few of us will discover the cure for cancer or be president of the United States, but everyone has opportunities to make a difference by helping someone else. You can do this at work, at home, at your church, or as a volunteer for a civic or charitable organization. To be most successful, start by examining your talents and passions. If you're good at something, you will tend to be more motivated and enthusiastic about it which will likely lead to more positive results that benefit others.

A great example of someone who succeeded with this method is Jerry Lewis, who is a great comedian and actor. Despite his success in the entertainment industry, I believe his most lasting contribution to the world is his fifty-year dedication to eliminating muscular dystrophy. Throughout his career he has used his talent and his passion to raise hundreds of millions of dollars to help Jerry's kids. What a legacy.

A number of years ago, I made a list of my strengths and talents and put it alongside a list of the causes and ideas that motivate me and my passions. Near the top of my list was my belief that students and young adults could benefit from understanding the importance of saving early in life and the power of compound interest. I was convinced that if students really understood the value of the discipline and regularity of saving and investing early in life, their financial futures would be considerably brighter. As a banker and financial planner, this was also in my area of expertise. I even had some experience in this area as I had previously gone to classrooms to explain to students the power of compound interest. Contemplating my passion, my experience, and my talents in the financial realm brought me to the conclusion I had both the motivation and the know-how to put together a book on this subject. Consequently, I wrote my first book and began giving seminars to students about this topic.

Between books sold and talks given to students groups, I've had the opportunity to influence the financial future of nearly twenty thousand young adults. When I wrote the book, my thought was that it would be a successful endeavor if even a small number of those students took my message to heart and made some minor financial behavioral changes to enhance their financial futures. Happily, I have had several students come to me years after hearing my talk or reading my book to tell me that my concepts changed their lives, in some cases by developing a career interest in finance and in other cases by developing a desire to begin saving and investing. This has been one way for me to make a difference. I believe there is a way that every one of us can make a positive difference in the world. Think about your talents and passion and examine your heart and you will find many ways to make a difference in the world.

Summary:

Perfecting talents and interests for uses that can help others is a way to make a difference in the world.

Workshop:
Make a difference in the world

Do you think this is an important truth? Why or why not?

Make a list of your talents and interests. Pay special attention to any that seem to intersect.

Do you know someone who volunteers often or does something else to make a difference in the world? How might your life be different if you follow their example?

Do you make an effort to regularly do things that will make a difference in the lives of others? Why or why not?

Look at the list you made above and write ways in which you can utilize your strengths and interests to start making a difference today. What will be difficult? What steps should you take to overcome those difficulties? (List plan or steps) What might change if you start doing this?

TRUTH
21

Get as Much Education as Possible

"Human history becomes more and more a race
between education and catastrophe."
—Wells, H.G. The Outline of History chapter 41

"The man who does not read good books has no advantage
over the man who can't read them."
—Mark Twain

"Education is not given for the purpose of earning a living; it is learning
what to do with the living after you earn it that counts."
—Abraham Lincoln

One of the best things you can do in your life to be personally and financially successful is commit to being a lifelong learner. Statistics show that more education on average means more lifetime earnings. I have read studies that show that every dollar spent on a person's education translates, on average, to 35 dollars of future lifetime earnings. Consequently, the income differential between a high school graduate and a college graduate continues to widen. In 1980, college graduates earned on average 25 percent more than high school graduates.

Today, that difference is 95 percent. According to the Census Bureau, the lifetime earnings differential between a high school graduate and a college graduate is 900,000 dollars.

According to the journal article "The Value of a College Degree" by Kathleen Porter, education, lifelong learning, and reading as much as possible will also enhance your written and verbal communication skills, analytical skills, and overall knowledge. All of these things will help you enjoy, understand, better appreciate, and contribute to the world around you. A study done by the Institute of Higher Education Policy showed that college graduates enjoy "higher levels of saving, increased personal and professional mobility, improved quality of life for their offspring, better consumer decision making, and more hobbies and leisure activities."

Our greatest leaders in almost every field are voracious readers, devouring book after book so that they can become better equipped to do their jobs. My reading shows that almost every president of the United States was a voracious reader, a trait which helped them better understand and appreciate the world around them and allowed them to make more informed decisions. In contrast, imagine a person with absolutely no education who could not read or write and could speak very little. How much could that person enjoy and appreciate life? Think how many things they would miss out on. I believe the more a person learns, the better he understands that life is wonderful, amazing, and precious.

Many people believe that once they are in the workforce their education is over, but this does not have to be the case.

For example, I knew a woman who earned all one hundred and twenty hours for her college degree while she worked at the bank. In my case, I decided to expand my education by pursuing a certified financial planning degree while serving as Chairman and CEO of the bank. By reading and studying a little each night, it took me three years, more than one thousand hours of study, and twenty-eight hours of testing to receive the degree. It was definitely worth it, though, because it has been useful to me in my second career which includes writing books, advising people on how to invest money, and giving seminars to help people with their finances.

Even now that I have completed both my degrees, it is interesting to me to read about all subjects, especially areas in which I have little previous knowledge. My belief is that generally being well read and educated makes a person more interesting and allows them to feel more comfortable in their interactions with almost anyone. To me, the value of being a lifelong learner far outweighs the time and effort you must put into it.

Summary:

In addition to increasing your abilities and lifetime earning power, learning and reading can be enjoyable, will broaden your perspectives, and will help you appreciate and participate in life to the fullest.

Workshop:
Get as much education as possible

Do you think this is an important truth? Why or why not?

What is the highest level of education that you hope to obtain? Do you think your life would be different if you got even more education than that? For example, if you are just hoping to graduate high school and get a job, how might your life be different if you go to college instead?

Think about the most educated person you know. Would their life be any different if they had less education? How?

Other than your required school work, do you make a conscious effort to learn new things on a regular basis? Why or why not?

What kinds of things can you do in your daily life to continue becoming more educated? What will be difficult? What steps should you take to overcome those difficulties? (List plan or steps) What might change if you do this?

TRUTH
22

Give and it will Come Back to You

"Give and it will come back to you, pressed down, shaken together, and running over."
—Luke 6:38

I believe that life is about loving God with all your heart, mind, and soul and then loving others. To love others, you must help them. Sharing, giving, and helping others will make your life fuller and much more satisfying. There are countless ways that you can go about doing this. Sometimes, a person's vocation may be helpful to others and, by doing their job well, they provide goods and/or services that benefit someone else. If that's not the case for you, you can also help a friend in need or volunteer for a non-profit organization, a church, or other charity. You can also help with a civic project or by doing something like coaching a baseball team or being a volunteer for a scouting organization. It is important to give of both your time and money, so when you're short on time you can use your money and resources to help those in need.

The fascinating thing about really giving is that you often get more back in return than you give. In my life, any cause that I have really dedicated myself to that helps others has always come back to help me in other ways. Sometimes I've gotten additional professional knowledge that has helped me in my career; other times I've made contacts with people who have been beneficial to me, and many times I've been given the opportunity to take on other challenges. All of these benefits are in addition to the satisfaction I get from making a positive difference.

For some reason that only God knows, my building skills and ability to fix mechanical problems are probably worse than nearly everyone else in the world. My wife and children will verify this. However, regardless of my inadequacy, I have volunteered several times to assist with building a Habitat for Humanity home in our town. On a couple of occasions when my children were growing up we all went together and made it a family outing. The rest of my family has normal skills in this area, so they get along fine helping to build these houses. On both of these occasions with my family, my attempts to build somehow resulted in near death experiences. In the worst accident, a large beam knocked me to the ground and cut my forehead somewhat severely. (My wife's one shortfall in life is that she seems to laugh hysterically when ever my actions result in my own injury.) In this case for me, this truth may be more appropriately stated as "give and it will hit you back." Luckily I was fine and I was still glad that I helped out. Those times were good family experiences and lasting memories in which the importance of giving was reinforced for my children. That in and of itself was a huge payback to me.

Eight to ten years ago, I decided to help out in a less dangerous capacity and I started volunteering to play the guitar and sing for the four-year-old and younger class that is held during our church service. I'm not a great guitar player or singer (although kids four years old and younger think I'm really good) but it helps the leaders in the class find ways to occupy the kids during the service. Additionally, the little kids all seem to enjoy it and will point at me out in public and say "there is Mr. Ed" and give me high fives when I finish singing. Although the little kids enjoy it, their delight is not nearly as much as mine. When I play for them it makes me feel good for the rest of the day. If I have to be gone for a week, I miss it. That is the way giving works.

Summary:
If a person gives of his talents, time, and money for the sole purpose of helping someone else, his gift will multiply back to him in ways he never expected.

Workshop:
Give and it will come back to you

Do you think this is an important truth? Why or why not?

Think of the last time you did something for someone else. Did you receive something in return? This could be something tangible, like an award or a gift, or something intangible like a feeling of accomplishment or goodwill. Was it worth it?

Think of the last time someone did something for you. What did that person receive in return? Do you think they are glad they helped you out?

Do you make an effort to give to others on a regular basis? Why or why not?

What can you do in your daily life to start giving back to others? What will be difficult? What steps should you take to overcome those difficulties? (List plan or steps) What might change if you start doing this?

TRUTH
23

You've Gotta Believe

"The only thing that really matters is faith expressing itself as love."
—Galatians 5:6

In my experience, belief in a higher power can change your whole perspective on life. If a person does not believe in a higher power, they often think that if no one sees what they do it doesn't matter. However, someone who believes in God recognizes that He knows everything they do, so there are no secrets and no hiding from their actions. This perspective encourages them to live an open, honest, and moral life. Christians like myself believe that the Holy Spirit lives inside us to guide and direct us in our everyday lives. For me, this direction is usually subtle, a feeling that I should do or say something to someone or sometimes not do or say something. Following this lead of the Holy Spirit impacts my decisions in my day-to-day life but seldom is this direction forceful or overwhelming.

Everyone's spiritual journey is different. Personally, I accepted Christ into my life the summer before my senior year in high school when I was in the hospital for a couple of weeks for a stomach ailment. The hospital stay was making me feel pretty low until my best friend's father brought me a Book of John, which moved me to ask Jesus into my life. Immediately, I was much more confident and motivated to do my best in everything. No longer was I satisfied with just getting by, which had been my standard operating procedure before. Additionally, my standard of integrity increased dramatically. My life changed drastically and, consequently, my college experience was successful in all areas, including academics, sports, and extracurricular activities and I was given the opportunities that led to my career. Accepting Christ into my life changed me back then, and continues to change me even now.

Many studies show that people who believe in a higher power are happier, live longer, and generally have a better outlook on life. I think this is because belief in God helps a person realize that their purpose in life is to love God, love others, and make the most of the talents God has given us to make the world a better place for others.

Several years ago, I had one of those rare but powerful communications from God that strengthened my faith and reinforced the concept that "you've gotta believe." Throughout the week before this experience, for whatever reason, I had been wondering, praying, and even worrying about what heaven would be like. One night late that week, a very powerful feeling awakened me in the middle of the night with answers to my question. A strong feeling compelled me to get out of bed immediately and go to the kitchen table to write down this answer. Within just a few seconds, without hesitation, and without thinking at all, I wrote several things on a piece of paper. I wrote that the components of heaven would be a reunion with loved ones, past family, and friends; a recap of my life, showing how it was meaningful and successful; an assurance that immediate family would be in heaven, my spouse, children, parents, and siblings; an overwhelming sense of love and uniting with love and our creator; and a call to a higher purpose to be meaningful and productive.

After writing this down, I went back to bed and, since this type of experience was rare and new, I began to wonder whether or not this message for me was really from God. I prayed to God and asked if there was a way He could somehow confirm this to me. Immediately, I felt strongly that I should turn to look at the clock, which read 2:07. In a very powerful way my spirit said that 2:07 meant "to heaven." For me, this was a confirmation that God had spoken to me in a very personal way.

Things like this are difficult to write out and explain because they are very personal. Since this was my spiritual moment, I'm not even sure it will mean something for everyone. However, it strengthened my faith and showed me that God can communicate to us sometimes in very powerful and mysterious ways. If you open your mind and heart, He will communicate with you in a way that means something to you and only you.

Summary:
Belief in God is the most important decision in a person's life.

Workshop:
You've gotta believe

Do you think this is an important truth? Why or why not?

Do you believe in a higher power? If so, how does that affect your everyday life? If not, do you think your life would be different if you did believe?

Think of someone in your life who is strong in their religious beliefs. How does that belief affect their day to day life and interactions with others?

How can you start building or strengthening your own personal relationship with God? What will be difficult? What steps should you take to overcome those difficulties? (List plan or steps) What might change if you do this?

TRUTH
24

Commit to Love One Person Forever

**"For this reason, a man will leave his father and mother and
be united to his wife and they will become one flesh."**
—Genesis 1:24

A few years ago, *Time* magazine did a study in which they asked people "What one thing in life brought you the greatest happiness?" The results showed that a person's spouse or marriage was one of the top three greatest sources of happiness for the respondents, along with enjoyment of a person's children and grandchildren and their religion. Other studies, such as ones done by Rand Research, have also shown that married people tend to live longer than single people. In one of their research briefs, the research company states that "numerous studies covering 140 years have shown that married persons tend to live longer than their unmarried counterparts." The reasons for this are numerous, but one key explanation is that couples who love each other provide support for each other in good times and bad, share their lives together, and become best friends. That constant companionship is invaluable.

Unfortunately, many people today are scared of the commitment of marriage because they are afraid of having a failed relationship. In my opinion, failed relationships don't have to happen. But, even if you are certain that failure is a possibility, I believe the old saying that "it is better to have loved and lost than never to have loved at all." My belief is that marriage is God's plan for most men and woman. For those who are considering marriage, the most critical part is obviously choosing the right spouse. One of my former tennis players, who was in a serious relationship with his girlfriend, recently asked me for advice on choosing the right spouse. The advice I gave him was the same advice I would give anyone in the same situation.

Most importantly, decide if you love the other person. It is difficult to describe how you will know you are in love, except to say that when you are in love, you will know it. Once you've decided you love them, there are a few other things to take into consideration. First, are they someone you feel you can always trust? This is vital because there can be no meaningful relationships without trust. Second, do you have similar religious beliefs? Opposing beliefs can make for a challenging marriage. Third, how did you both feel about a family? It can be a serious problem if one person wants children and the other does not. Finally, are you on similar intellectual and/or educational levels? A spouse should be your best friend and someone with whom you can share and discuss ideas, aspirations, thoughts, and feelings. A large gap in intellectual activity could make meaningful communication difficult. These were all questions

I considered before asking Marla to marry me and, thirty-four years later, I can still say that marrying her was the best decision of my life. Our love for each other grows deeper each year. She is my best friend and we enjoy life together.

Once you find your potential spouse, it's important to recognize that marriage is a commitment that takes work. If you are not ready for that, wait to get married until you are. It seems to me that some people can be too quick to give up on a relationship when there is a problem. For Marla and me, ending our marriage to solve a problem has never been an option or even a consideration. Instead, we work to solve the problem together and make the relationship work.

Having a spouse to share life with can make all your experiences better. During my college years, I had a great summer job taking statistics that allowed me to travel all over the country with the Kansas City Royals baseball team. This was a great opportunity to see many different towns all over the country, but I don't think it was nearly as fun by myself as it would've been if I could've shared it with someone I loved. Sharing life's experiences with the person you love most in the world is a wonderful part of life. I can't imagine enjoying any part of my life nearly as much without Marla.

Summary:
Life is much more enjoyable if you can find one special person to love and share it with.

Workshop:
Commit tu love one person forever

Do you think this is an important truth? Why or why not?

If you are in a long term committed relationship, do you think it makes your life better? Why or why not? If you're not in a committed relationship, how do you think your life would be affected if you were?

Talk to a married couple that you know. Do they think their relationship has affected their lives for the better? How?

What might be difficult about maintaining a long term, committed relationship? What steps should you take to overcome those difficulties? (List or plan steps) What might change in your life if you do this?

TRUTH
25

Spend Time With Your Family

"The cats in the cradle and the silver spoon, little boy blue and the man and the moon. When you coming home Dad, I don't when, but we'll get together then son, you know we'll have a good time then."
—"Cats in the Cradle" by Harry Chapin

It's easy to get caught up in life and overlook things that are really important. Building careers, making money, making ends meet, pursing hobbies, relaxing, and unwinding all get in the way of one of the best investments of time you can make—spending quality time with your family. I have never heard anyone say later in life that they spent too much time with their family, but many people look back and wish they had rearranged their priorities and spent more time with their family. Try to carve out more time to enjoy with your spouse, children, and family, loving them, helping to mold and develop them, and sharing life with them.

When I married Marla, I made a conscious decision to always place my family first and spend as much quality time with them as possible. That way, when we had children, my decision was already made regarding my priorities. Now that my children are grown, I have no regrets about not spending enough time with them. I have many fun, lasting memories with them as kids, especially because Marla and I felt it was important to attend nearly every game and activity of our three kids. Since we had already decided attendance was mandatory, I chose to make myself useful and ended up coaching many of my children's sports, including the boys' high school tennis team. From the time they were very young, I hit tennis balls with the kids regularly and took them to tournaments and lessons. Some of the best periods of quality time I had with them were spent driving to out of town tournaments and lessons (in my daughter's case it was dance lessons) because it provided uninterrupted time to talk. In addition to being involved in their everyday lives, Marla and I felt it was very important to take an annual vacation with the kids. Vacations can be expensive, but they don't have to be. They're just a planned get away in which the family spends time together to do something special and memorable. No matter where you go be sure to take plenty of pictures and/or videos—this is an important part of making memories. On one trip to New York City, I took about a hundred pictures of the city and my family. When I developed them, I saw that my middle child, Aaron, who was probably sixteen at the time, had rolled his head back with his eyes closed and his mouth open in every picture. Boy was I mad, but today we all laugh about it. It is a memory, too.

As CEO at the bank, it was important to me to be sure my staff knew I thought that family was more important than work. To reinforce this concept, I encouraged them to take time from work to attend important family events, like their children's Christmas plays. I expected the staff to help each other out and cover for their co-workers so everyone could attend their own children's plays and other important family events.

Time goes by quickly and it is easy to say you can't make it to this ball game or play but you'll make it to the next one. Unfortunately, there will always be a reason to put what is important off again and again until it's too late. Find a way to fit it into your schedule now.

Summary:
Spending time with family is possibly the best investment a person can make in life.

Workshop:
Spend time with your family

Do you think this is an important truth? Why or why not?

Imagine that you are ten years in the future. Do you think you would regret not spending enough time with your family? Why or why not?

List some activities that you think would be fun for you to do as a family.

Do you make a conscious effort to spend time with your family? Why or why not? Do you think this affects your life in anyway? How?

Look at the list you made on the left. How can you start incorporating some of these things into your day to day life so that you spend more time with your family? What will be difficult? What steps should you take to overcome those difficulties? (List plan or steps) What might change if you do this?

TRUTH
Plus One
All You Need is Love

There's Nothing you can do that can't be done. There's nothing you can sing that can't be sung...all you need is love, all you need is love, love is all you need." —All You Need is Love, The Beatles

"For God so loved the world that he gave his only begotten Son, that whosoever believes in him, shall not perish, but have eternal life." —John 3:16

"...no greater love is this than a man lay down his life for another." —John 15:12

"...God is love. Whoever lives in love lives in God, and God is in him." —1 John 4:16

"Love is patient, love is kind. It does not envy, it does not boast, it is not proud. It is not rude, it is not self seeking, it is not easily angered, it keeps no record of wrongs. Love does not delight in evil but rejoices with the truth. It always protects, always trusts, always hopes, always perseveres....And now these three remain; faith, hope and love. But the greatest of these is love." —1 Corinthians 4-7, 13

> "'Love your God with all your heart and all your soul and with all your mind.' This is the first and greatest commandment. And the second is like it. 'Love your neighbor as yourself.' All the Law and the Prophets hang on these two commandments." —Matthew 22: 37-40

I've been asked several times since first writing my original list of 25 Truths, if I ever felt the need to add to my list of truths. In other words, did I miss any truths? Even after the original publication of 25 Truths, my answer to this question as always been an emphatic "no". From the beginning I have always felt that the list was complete-at least for me, and that 25 was just the right number.

Then just before the republication of this book by Harrison House, I suddenly knew that I had missed an obvious truth that encapsulates all the other 25-a summary of everything. Hence, instead of Truth 26, I call this plus one, a summation of what is really important in life, plain and simple-love.

Many times during times of tragedy, people love and compassion for others shines through in exemplary and an unexpected ways. In some of these situations people risk and sometimes sacrifice their lives for others. Last year the city of Joplin, Missouri, which is a several hour drive from my home, experienced an F-5 tornado that was one of the deadliest and most destructive in the history of our country. Marla and I and our oldest son happened to drive through Joplin on the way back from a wedding just a few short hours before the storm hit. This massive tornado, with winds in excess of 200 mph, leveled business, schools and hospital as well as 4000 homes in a six mile long and at some point one mile wide path through the center of town, killing 162 people.

A week after the storm, I went a group from my church down to Joplin to help with the clean up. The destruction was immense but the attitude of the people who lived there was uplifting. I talked to several people who had lost their home and all their possessions and they all felt blessed to be alive. These survivors could not believe the outpouring of love and help (food, water, money, supplies and clean up) that was being offered by others. We heard numerous stories of love and compassion and courage. One of these stories was repeated by the President of the United States in a memorial service held in Joplin. This involved the manager of the Pizza Hut, a building which had been not far from where I worked on clean up. When the manager learned that the tornado was heading his way, he directed all the customers and staff in the building into a heavy metal freezer inside the Pizza Hut. Unfortunately the door wouldn't stay shut and the storm was ripping people out of the freezer. The manger took action and wrapped a bungee cable around his arm trying to keep it the freezer door shut while everyone else was moved to the back of the freezer. According to a employee of the manager, when the brunt of the tornado hit, the manager tried to hold the door shut but the door finally blew open taking the door and the manager up into the funnel but leaving the freezer. The 19 people that were in the freezer all survived from the manager's efforts, but the manager himself was sucked up into the storm and killed. One of his employees in the freezer said "the only reason we survived is because he held the door shut with a strap". The Pizza Hut manager, a father of two children with a third on the way, gave his life for others exemplifying "no greater love is this than a man lay down his life for others."

One of the strongest feelings of love I believe a person can feel is the love a parent feels for his children, which begins at birth. The miracle of birth combined with the love a parent feels is overwhelming. Marla and I have been blessed with this feeling three times with three wonderful children. I was most recently reminded of this feeling with the birth of our first grandchild, London Beth Douglas. It is quite a feeling to see how much my son Aaron and his wife Micah (along with London's Uncle Jared and Aunt Kaylee) love her and of course Marla and I feel the same. Holding her and singing to her (which I do) is a joy that is indescribable. There is not a question that London's parents and grandparents would do anything for that child even if it meant giving their lives for her. In a small way, I think the love a parent has for a child allows us to understand and appreciate how much God loves us, his children. "For God so loved the world that he gave his only begotten son ..."

Nothing a person accomplishes, or does or says matters the least without love. God is love and it is the culmination and completion of everything we are, we do or we say. Practice the other 25 Truths with love or they won't work.

Summary:

If I could sum all the truths into one it is "Love". Do everything with true love towards God and man and everything else will come together.

About the Author

Ed Douglas retired at the beginning of 2006 from Citizens Bancshares Bank, headquartered in Chillicothe, Missouri, after nearly thirty-two years with the company. He spent his last twenty years as president and, later, chairman and CEO. Under his leadership, the company grew its capital and increased assets over tenfold to a 1,000,000,000 dollar bank holding company with locations in twenty-five towns. His current title is Chairman Emeritus and Board Member of Citizens Bancshares. He is a Certified Financial Planner and currently operates Ed Douglas Certified Financial Planning/Consulting.

Ed is the author of two other books, *Making a Million with Only $2000: Every Young Person Can Do It,* currently in it's second printing, and *The Money Marathon: 7 Simple Steps to Financial Freedom.* He regularly gives seminars to adults and students on important financial topics as well as seminars on topics of character, values, and virtue.

Ed has been appointed by three different governors in Missouri to statewide positions, including Commissioner of the Missouri Highway and Transportation Commission and President of the Northwest Missouri State University Board of Regents. He currently serves on the William Jewell College Board, a number of local civic boards, and is an active member of his local church, Cornerstone Church.

He has coached the high school tennis team for the last fifteen years and is a member of the Fifty States Marathon Club, having run sixteen marathons in fifteen states. He and his wife Marla reside in Chillicothe and have three children, Jared, Aaron, and Kaylee, one daughter-in-law, Aaron's wife Micah, and one granddaughter, London Beth.

PRAYER OF SALVATION

God loves you—no matter who you are, no matter what your past. God loves you so much that He gave His one and only begotten Son for you. The Bible tells us that "...whoever believes in him shall not perish but have eternal life" (John 3:16 NIV). Jesus laid down His life and rose again so that we could spend eternity with Him in heaven and experience His absolute best on earth. If you would like to receive Jesus into your life, say the following prayer out loud and mean it from your heart.

Heavenly Father, I come to You admitting that I am a sinner. Right now, I choose to turn away from sin, and I ask You to cleanse me of all unrighteousness. I believe that Your Son, Jesus, died on the cross to take away my sins. I also believe that He rose again from the dead so that I might be forgiven of my sins and made righteous through faith in Him. I call upon the name of Jesus Christ to be the Savior and Lord of my life. Jesus, I choose to follow You and ask that You fill me with the power of the Holy Spirit. I declare that right now I am a child of God. I am free from sin and full of the right-eousness of God. I am saved in Jesus' name. Amen.

If you prayed this prayer to receive Jesus Christ as your Savior for the first time, please contact us on the Web at **www.harrisonhouse.com** to receive a free book.

Or you may write to us at
Harrison House • P.O. Box 35035 • Tulsa, Oklahoma 74153

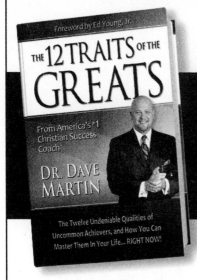

The Harrison House Vision

Proclaiming the truth and the power

Of the Gospel of Jesus Christ

With excellence;

Challenging Christians to

Live victoriously,

Grow spiritually,

Know God intimately.